SHAKING THE FAMILY TREE

Donna,

  May God richly bless
your family.

  Bill

Shaking The Family Tree

Dr. William B. Berman
Dr. Dale R. Doty
Jean Huff Graham

VICTOR BOOKS.

A DIVISION OF SCRIPTURE PRESS PUBLICATIONS INC.
USA CANADA ENGLAND

Unless otherwise noted, Scripture quotations are from the *Holy Bible, New International Version,* © 1973, 1978, 1984, International Bible Society. Used by permission of Zondervan Bible Publishers. Others are from the *King James Version* (KJV); *The Amplified New Testament* (AMP), © 1954, 1958, the Lockman Foundation; the *New American Standard Bible* (NASB), © the Lockman Foundation 1960, 1962, 1963, 1968, 1971, 1972, 1973, 1975, 1977; and *The Living Bible* (TLB), © 1971, Tyndale House Publishers, Wheaton, Illinois 60189. Used by permission.

Library of Congress Cataloging-in-Publication Data

Berman, Wm. B. (William B.)
    Shaking the family tree: using your family's past to strengthen your
family's future / by Wm. B. Berman, Dale R. Doty, and Jean Huff Graham.
      p.   cm.
    Includes bibliographical references.
    ISBN 0-89693-891-3
    1. Family–Psychological aspects. 2. Marriage–Psychological aspects.
3.Parenting–Psychological aspects. 4. Family–Religious life. I. Doty,
Dale R. II. Graham, Jean Huff. III. Title.
HQ518.B468 1991
306.85 – dc20
                                        91-3307
                                          CIP

---

1 2 3 4 5 6 7 8 9 10 Printing/Year 95 94 93 92 91

CONTENTS

*This book is affectionately dedicated
to our families, both past and present,
who have taught us, encouraged us, and
patiently borne our mistakes as
we learned the truths we share in
these pages.*

TABLE OF ILLUSTRATIONS

BEFORE YOU READ
THIS BOOK

This book is about change. It asks you, the reader, to take a serious look at your family beliefs, values, and attitudes which have passed down from generation to generation. It then asks you to take a courageous step forward to change the ineffective, and possibly damaging, beliefs, values, and attitudes that you discover.

We believe that those readers who follow the steps and suggestions found in this book will gain insight into their own family system. They will realize answers to questions they have been unable, until now, to ask: why certain things cause them to react; why they behave in ways that they would rather not; why they can't be loving spouses and parents when they want to so badly.

But insight and answers aren't enough; change requires action, and change in a family system takes time, patience, and courage. It may mean rocking a boat that seems precariously balanced on an already stormy sea. For some, it may mean seeking professional help for problems that have existed too long for self-help solutions. Many readers, however, will discover the basics of a healthy system already in place. These readers need only fine tune their marriage and parenting skills to have a family that meets the scriptural ideals.

It is our prayer that as you read you will find encouragement through Scripture and courage through the indwelling Holy Spirit. We pray that you will, by faith, take action to bring health to your family system and add God's blessing to the generations to come.

THE AUTHORS

PART ONE

"Remember the days of old; consider the generations long past. Ask your father and he will tell you, your elders, and they will explain to you."

Deuteronomy 32:7

CHAPTER ONE

LEFTOVERS, FLIP-FLOPS, AND FAMILY TREES

"No, Mother, not until you say please!"

Jeffrey folded his arms, a defiant expression frozen on his 11-year-old face. His mother sat holding a list of rules and consequences drawn up at our suggestion. She had completed the task successfully. Jeffrey, however, did not share her enthusiasm. He met her demand that he sign the paper with a challenge of his own.

We waited as mother and son vied for the position of authority. In the end, the mother weakened, submitted to her son's demands, and said, "Please."

Jeffrey signed the paper, but his message was clear: A rule is a rule only if I give my permission.

Dismissing Jeffrey from the session, we turned to his mother, Helen. Tears ran down her cheeks.

"I thought I had this all worked out," she began. "I've been in therapy before." Helen went on to relate painful memories from her own childhood, ending with the infamous "Mother's Curse": When you have children, I hope they treat you the same way you treat me.

THE PROBLEM WITH LEFTOVERS

Helen was discovering what so many of us already know: Parenting is a tough job. It doesn't pay well, the hours are terrible, and often the benefits seem nonexistent. To make matters worse, we all carry emotional baggage left over from our own childhood, and these "leftovers" can haunt us as we face our responsibilities as parents. Times of unresolved grief, abusive incidents, and major family fights make an indelible imprint on our minds. These issues may surface later and create problems in our marriages and with our children.

It often makes no difference whether we suffered as the victim of these events ourselves, as in Helen's case, or whether we observed a close relative's trials. Donna, a stable and well-adjusted wife and mother, enjoyed a close relationship with her husband and three children. She found herself, however, increasingly at odds with her 14-year-old daughter, Jessica.

In reaction to Jessica's teenaged independence, Donna became overly protective. As a result, Jessica pulled away from her mother, causing Donna to increase her attempts to control Jessica's behavior. A look into Donna's background revealed that her younger sister became promiscuous around the age of 14 or 15, and subsequently had a child out of wedlock.

Donna's problems with Jessica resulted from an anniversary reaction, another example of a leftover issue. Problems often occur around the anniversary date of certain events, especially if those events carry with them a profound emotional impact.

NO EXPERIENCE NECESSARY

Parenting, one of the most important and difficult jobs in any society, traditionally required only two things: fertility and intercourse. Medical science now eliminates even these in some cases. Many jobs of lesser significance demand stringent training programs and are protected from unqualified individuals performing them. But parenting has no such safeguards.

Most of us learned to be parents by using our own parents as models, even though we pledged never to raise our children the way we were raised. Free and often contradictory advice from well-meaning friends, relatives, and talk-show guests add to our confusion. Even Scripture does not provide us with practical solutions to common parenting problems such as homework, allowances, or bed-wetting. To further complicate matters, changing societal values result in ever-increasing rates of divorce, single parenting, and stepfamilies. These "recast" families share a unique set of problems. They must adjust their roles and remold the shape of their lives together.

In the end, parenting remains a skill learned mainly through trial and error. This method, however, turns the oldest child into a guinea pig, and by the time child number three or four comes along, we often discover that though our wisdom may be greater, we're too tired to care.

WHEN EVERYTHING ISN'T ENOUGH

Many parents share the experience of trying all the suggestions for behavior management from the latest child guidance book, only to have each new method fail. What do parents do when they've tried everything and their children are still uncontrollable? Or what if a parent is constantly at odds with one particular child, or is equally guilty of uncontrollable behavior (such as anger)? Is this person just a "bad" parent? We share the opinion that most parents truly want the best for their children but lack an understanding of why they respond as they do to their children and mates.

Most parenting books teach specific tools for managing problem behavior—what to do about temper tantrums or how to establish a bedtime routine, for example. Unfortunately, they offer no help to parents in understanding why they are unable to apply such tools consistently. We recognize the need for behavior management tools, and plan to address them in later chapters, but we also recognize the importance of the attitudes and actions of past generations in determining whether or not we raise emotionally healthy children. If we grew up in a well-functioning family, we may do a good job ourselves as parents. On the other hand, if our family of origin did not function successfully, we may find ourselves repeating the dysfunctional process with our own children. Consequently, a study of our family system can offer valuable clues for overcoming ineffectual parenting methods and becoming more capable parents.

BEATING THE SYSTEM

A family system consists of a nuclear family group (husband, wife, and children) and the past three to seven generations in the families of both husband and wife. A study of your family system helps you determine where your beliefs about families originated, and can aid in creating a successful marriage and in rearing well-adjusted children.

Family systems theory looks at the way a family functions by studying the structure of that family: what role each member plays within the system, and what rules govern how that family functions in day-to-day life.

In family systems, relationships between members are as important in determining behavior as the individual temperaments and personalities of the members. Family members interact and influence one another, constantly reacting to changes in the life cycle which repeats with each new generation. Since the entire family shares the responsibility of problems within the system, healthy family systems have a better chance of producing healthy, well-behaved children.

Individuals participate in a variety of systems, such as church, school, and work, during the course of a lifetime. However, the family is the most important and the most influential system any of us will encounter. Profound and lasting impressions become etched on the mind of a child as he or she grows up in this vital system, and these impressions do not disappear with the coming of adulthood.

FLIP-FLOPS

Most of us can describe in great detail the things we do not want to do as our parents did. We know for certain what we disliked in our own family of origin; we are less clear about what we must do differently to truly break free of those patterns. The usual answer to this dilemma is to swing to the opposite extreme of our parents' actions.

For example, Marla's parents fought in a cruel, demeaning way. As a child, Marla hated listening to these fights and made a decision deep within never to argue when she married. Instead, she developed a pattern of withdrawing in silence when things became tense. She refused to confront any issue. On the surface, Marla appeared to be a peacemaker, but in reality she and her husband left important issues unsettled and allowed emotions to fester.

Henry's parents spanked him in anger to the point of physical abuse. As a consequence, Henry determined never to strike his own child. He discovered, however, that not doing something is only half the solution. A flip-flop to extreme permissiveness, with no external controls applied to a child's behavior, is as unhealthy as a parent's angry abuse. Neither Marla nor Henry had any idea what to do differently. In both cases, when pushed to the end of their tolerance, they automatically resorted to the type of behavior with which they were most familiar: Henry struck out at his son in anger; Marla yelled abusively at her husband.

Reactionary parenting—going to the opposite extreme of our own parents—sets us up for failure. In the end, like Marla and Henry, we become like our parents and pass on to the next generation the very things we hated. Our spouses struggle with the same tendencies and if their family structure differed from our own, agreement over raising our children may seem difficult, if not impossible, to achieve.

I'M OK, BUT YOU'RE A LITTLE STRANGE

The place to begin understanding our actions of the present is in the past, taking a look at the generations which came before us. Studying the dynamics of our family system reveals the unquestioned beliefs and values we bring with us into family life. All too often this study also reveals a familiarity with unhealthy relationships, causing us to seek out mates who will recreate for us the same circumstances with which we are so well acquainted.

The family system's beliefs and values create a mindset, a way of looking at the world that gives us an image of a normal family—what each member looks like, how they act, what they do. We tend to assume that everyone sees "normal" the same way we see it. (Except our spouses, of course. Their families were weird, but ours were normal.) However, as we shall learn in chapter 3, wide variations of family functioning exist and unwillingness to allow for such variations can cause problems in both marriage and parenting. Though expression may differ from family to family, some basic characteristics of healthy families do exist.

THE JUNE CLEAVER SYNDROME

Well-functioning families grow from strong marriages which begin with a successful launching from their families of origin. Through good communication, the new husband and wife merge their ideas on family and parenting and create a unique parenting style consistent with God's mandates in Scripture. They become the glue which holds the rest of the family together, anticipating each new stage of the life cycle. As their children grow, they make decisions together about parenting, constantly blending their expectations and goals for their family. The couple enjoys a fulfilling relationship built on teamwork and mutual respect. They launch their own children into new marriages and can rejoice at the independence they forged into the lives of the next generation.

Sound like a 1950s sitcom? A rerun of "Ozzie and Harriet" or "Leave It To Beaver"? As unachievable as it may seem, we believe God desires that every family have its house in order, so that parents truly become the pride of their children (Proverbs 17:6).

PLAN B

Adam and Eve had a perfect relationship in a perfect environment until they developed a taste for apples. Because of Adam's sin, we all suffer from a broken relationship with God. But God's plan included the redemption of fallen man. His Son, Jesus Christ, provides that redemption for all who believe in Him. This process of redemption not only reclaims man for God, but also reclaims man's relationships with others. God gives us guidance in His Word, and wisdom through His Spirit, on how to conduct our relationships properly.

God planned that parenting should be a dual responsibility of two parents: a mother and a father bound together in a marital relationship. He illustrated this with the birth of His only Son. Mary could have gone to Bethlehem with a girlfriend and become a single parent, but God chose to place Jesus in a two-parent family. This is not to suggest that single parenting is less virtuous or less noble. Single parents face a difficult task, but one for which God's grace is sufficient. A closer look at the special needs of single- and stepparents comes in a later chapter.

Literature on the healthy family echoes the truth in God's instructions to families written thousands of years ago. The need for structure in the family, the authority of the parents over the children, relationships based on unconditional love — all of these commands God set forth in the Bible for our benefit.

God has field-tested His plan for over two thousand years and it works. In order to reap the blessings of this plan, however, we must each decide how much of His plan we are willing to understand and implement. As the Children of Israel discovered in going forth to possess the Promised Land, they could travel far and possess much or travel little and possess little (Joshua 1:3).

IT'S ONLY A STAGE

To travel forth into God's promised land for the family, we must look backward at the past to see where our family system has been and also learn what to expect in the years ahead. The life cycle of every family is a crucial issue. Those family units which cannot prepare for and adapt to the inevitable changes in their family life face the possibility of severe relationship problems.

Though the life cycle can be broken down many ways, most families typically experience these major stages: marriage; pregnancy; birth of first child and adjustments to parenthood; first child beginning school; adolescence; launching children into adulthood and marriages of their own; empty nest; retirement; and widowhood.

Families with many children may be in several of these stages at the same time, and "recast" families may find themselves going through them in a different order; however, if you have children, you are likely to go through each stage at some time in the life of your family.

Scripture facilitates moving through the family life cycle. By adhering to God's principles, the family can successfully negotiate each stage. A breakdown in any stage along the way affects all later stages. The tasks of each stage are discussed more thoroughly in the chapters which follow.

LEFTOVERS AGAIN?

Along with the expected stages of family development, any number of unexpected transitions may occur. Crisis situations such as severe illnesses, accidents, divorce and premature deaths can throw a family into upheaval.

Problems within the family typically appear at transition points when members are moving from one stage into the next. Leftover issues complicate adjustments to new stages. Before dealing with present issues, therefore, we must search for leftovers, seeking to understand their influence on our family life and parenting styles. We can be victims of our families or we can profit from them. They can be a source of strength or a source of weakness. What we do with leftover issues, once we become aware of them, determines whether we make positive use of our childhood experiences or negative use of them. In the next two chapters we will put on a pair of bifocal glasses. First, we will look through the top lens into the distance of your family history. Then we will look more closely at the family in which you grew up.

FAMILY TREES

Where did your parents come from? What influenced you to choose a particular mate? Why do you react to your children in the way you do? The answers to these questions and many more can be found in your family tree. But not just any family tree. This tree is more than just a genealogy; it is a way of looking through past generations for patterns and traditions. Called a *genogram*, its branches hold the secrets of the past that shaped your character and made you who you are.

WORDS TO THE WARY
Because the family system concept may be new to you, we suggest that you read through this entire book before you attempt to complete any of the exercises in the next few chapters, and especially before you try any of the behavior management techniques explained later. Once you are comfortably familiar with this concept, we urge you to go back through the book slowly, and do each project as thoroughly as you can. Each step is important in developing a plan for establishing a healthy family system which will benefit your own children and be a legacy for generations to come.

CHAPTER TWO

ECHOES FROM THE PAST

Traditions play an important part in any family system. Those rituals which always occur on certain occasions form a fence of security around each member, giving him or her a sense of family and self. But not all traditions have such positive effects. Some traditional ways of thinking and behaving can be detrimental to the functioning of the family system.

COMING TO TERMS WITH TRADITIONS

Bob Petterson, pastor of Christ Presbyterian Church in Tulsa, Oklahoma, tells a story about an Eskimo family. A father and his young son were pulling the elderly grandfather on a sled, taking him out onto the ice to die, in obedience to a longstanding tradition of their tribe.

After leaving the old man and the sled, the father and son began to walk back to their village. Suddenly, the young boy turned around and ran back to his grandfather who, having already shed his fur robe, had moved away from the sled and sat down on the ice.

The young boy picked up the rope and began pulling the sled back to where his father stood.

The father, not understanding the boy's actions, asked his son why he had gone back for the sled. The boy replied, "When you are old, I will use it to pull you out onto the ice."

The father thought for a long moment, then reached over and took the rope from his son's hand. Pulling the sled behind him, he went back to get the old man and take him home.

Like this Eskimo father and son, each of us comes out of a family that came out of a family that came out of a family. We have a history, and that history shapes the way we view the world. It determines what will seem usual and customary to us. Our past exerts an influence on us, causing us to do things without questioning or evaluating them. Even when we suspect that something is not quite right about our actions, we still tend to follow along in the same direction as the generations which came before us.

THE SINS OF THE FATHERS

The patterns and traditions once followed by many tribes and nationalities seem shocking and cruel to us today. But many, more subtle patterns exist, and although we may not display them for the world to see, we often unknowingly participate in them. Patterns such as physical abuse, alcoholism, mental illness, and sexual immorality, as well as anger and withdrawal, illustrate for us the truth of Exodus 34:7: "He does not leave the guilty unpunished; He punishes the children and their children for the sin of the fathers to the third and fourth generation." As an observation of a unique process, this verse cautions us about the longlasting consequences of our sins. In families with a history of abuse, the effect often extends to as many as seven generations.

Does this mean we are trapped—left with no way out? Absolutely not! God never leaves us stranded. He promises in 1 Corinthians 10:13 always to provide a way out of temptation, in this case, the temptation to repeat harmful family patterns. God shows us the way out of this dilemma in Leviticus 26:40-41: "But if they will confess their sins and *the sins of their fathers* . . . when their uncircumcised hearts are humbled and they pay for their *sin,* I will remember My covenant" (emphases added).

To pay for our *sin* (the sin nature inherited from Adam) we must believe on the name of Jesus who paid the penalty of sin for us all (John 1:12). Confessing our *fathers' sins* means agreeing with God about the sinful acts our forefathers committed, whether or not they recognized their acts as sinful. When God remembers His covenant, He restores us as though we had never sinned. "I will restore them because I have compassion on them. They will be as though I had not rejected them, for I am the Lord their God and I will answer them" (Zechariah 10:6).

THE RESTORATION PROCESS
The restoration process begins with salvation—acknowledging our helplessness and believing in Christ, accepting His sacrifice on our behalf. It continues with confessing our own sins, our acts of disobedience and distrust against God. Only then are we able to confess the sins of our forefathers. However, to accomplish this, we must first learn what those sins were and how they affect us and our children today. When we do this, God frees us to make the changes necessary in our family's structure and habits and thereby to break the influence of the past over us. Though God may initiate the process by giving insight, insight is never enough to produce change. It falls to each of us to take action—often painful and difficult—to bring change to our family system. For this, we must rely on the strengthening power of the Holy Spirit.

In Exodus 20:5, God promises to show "love to a thousand generations of those who love Me and keep My commandments." With this promise of blessings on a thousand generations in the future, we begin our journey into the past.

CHARTING THE PAST
In this chapter and the next, we introduce you to two tools for examining the history of your family system. The first is the genogram, a fancy name for a special kind of family tree. In addition to the usual names and dates, the genogram allows for notation of many other pertinent facts. It shows each family member in relationship to the others and provides a way to examine the nature of these relationships.

Genograms are drawn in such a way as to look at the family systems of both the husband and the wife in a nuclear family. Each family member is indicated by a box or circle: boxes represent males, circles represent females. Beside each box or circle, you record the name of the individual, and his or her present age is written inside. An X through the box or circle indicates death, with the person's age at the time of death superimposed on the X [see figure 1].

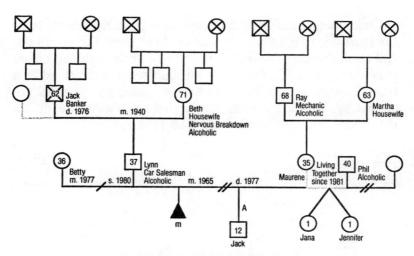

Figure 1. Genogram Symbols

Marriages are indicated by connecting a box and circle with solid lines, with the marriage date on the line. Affairs or living-together arrangements are shown by dashes instead of solid lines. Separations and divorces are signified by slashes across the marriage line: one for separation and two for divorce.

In families with multiple marriages, draw the different marriages from left to right. If both partners have had more than one marriage, the husband's successive marriages are drawn to the left, the wife's to the right [see figure 2].

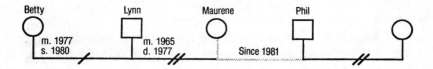

Figure 2. Symbols for Marriage, Separation, and Divorce

Children are indicated by drawing a birth line down from the marriage line, using a box or circle to show the sex of the child and drawing them in the order of birth with the oldest child on the left. Miscarriages and abortions are indicated by a triangle with either M or A beside. Adopted children are shown by adding an A to the birth line. Twins are drawn extending from the same birth line [see figure 3].

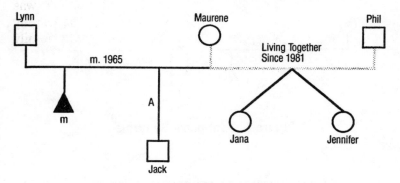

Figure 3. Symbols for Children

After drawing the basic genogram structure, add the birth dates, marriage dates, and death dates where applicable; write in where the person lives, or lived, his or her occupation, and educational level. Information about the person's emotional and medical history provides useful insight into the way that person functioned in society. Record successful functioning as well as failures.

Next comes research into the family life cycle and transition points. When did moves or job changes, etc., occur? What else happened in the family at the same time? Record all critical life events. You may need to use a separate sheet of paper for this. Be sure to include dates, if possible. After completing this phase of the genogram, which may take quite a lot of digging if the family history is unknown, analyze each relationship represented on the genogram, studying it for closeness or conflict. These can be noted on the genogram by joining the boxes and circles with three parallel lines to represent extreme closeness (≡ ≡), or zig-zags to represent conflictual relationships (⋀⋀). Notice sibling position by birth order and sex. Genograms typically include at least three generations. The more generations you can show on your genogram, the more insight you gain from it.

A LESSON FROM THE PAST

To illustrate the process of creating a genogram, we will map out for you the family of Joseph, the son of Jacob, who was sold into slavery by his brothers at the age of 17. The family history is found in Genesis 11–50. Joseph's nuclear family would look like the family shown in figure 4.

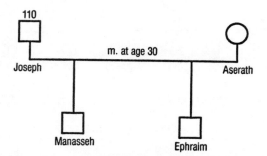

Figure 4. Joseph's Nuclear Family Genogram

This genogram shows that Joseph was married to Asenath and had two sons, Manasseh and Ephraim. We know that Joseph was 30 years old when he married Asenath and entered Pharoah's service. He lived 110 years. If we add a third generation to the genogram, along with Joseph's siblings, the diagram grows to the one seen in figure 5.

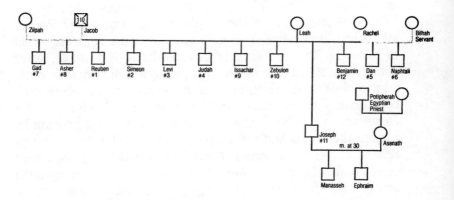

Figure 5. Three-generation Genogram for Joseph

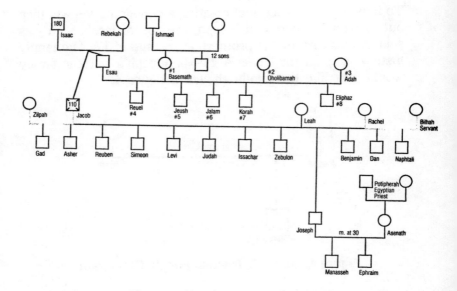

Figure 6. Four-generation Genogram for Joseph

Joseph was the 11th of 12 sons born to Jacob. Because of the nature of Jacob's marriages and the birth of sons to his wives' handmaidens, it is difficult to show the births in their natural order, so we have numbered them. The dashes show that Jacob had sons by Zilpah and Bilhah, though he was never married to them. The family begins to get interesting when we add a fourth generation [see figure 6].

This diagram shows that Jacob had a twin brother named Esau, and they were the sons of Isaac and Rebekah. Isaac had a half-brother named Ishmael who married and had 12 sons and at least one daughter, Basemath, who later married Esau.

The final genogram shows the full family tree with six generations represented [see figure 7].

Because of the intermarriages within the family, it is necessary to cross the marriage line of Abraham and Sarah to show Bethuel's family. Genograms of many generations may become complicated, especially when multiple marriages occur. In cases such as these, try different ways to get the genogram on one page. No absolutely correct method exists.

PATTERNS OF THE PAST

When we begin to analyze the genogram and history of Joseph, a number of interesting issues pop up. Though it makes a fascinating study, we mention only two such patterns here before giving you a list of questions to help you analyze your own family. You may want to practice on Joseph's family before diagramming your own, searching for other patterns within the generations.

Starting with Abraham, the pattern of deceit shows up in each succeeding generation. For instance, Abraham twice passed Sarah off as his sister (a half-truth) in order to escape being murdered. Isaac, Abraham's son, followed suit and lied about Rebekah being his sister. When Jacob came along he deceived Isaac and stole Esau's birthright and blessing. Then Laban, Jacob's father-in-law, deceived Jacob by giving him Leah in marriage rather than Rachel. Imagine Jacob's surprise when he awoke in the morning with the wrong woman in his bed! Jacob's sons lied to him about Joseph's death, and

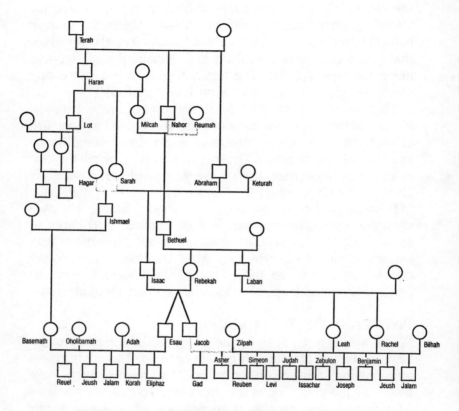

Figure 7. Six-generation Genogram for Joseph

then Joseph tricked them all into bringing Benjamin to Egypt.

The relationships between each generation also offer some valuable insight into this family. Abraham obviously favored Isaac, the child of God's covenant. Isaac in turn favored Esau, but Rebekah favored Jacob. Jacob was partial to Rachel, which made Leah jealous and started a baby boom. Jacob also showed great partiality to Joseph, who was Rachel's firstborn, and triggered the jealousy of Joseph's brothers and their eventual plotting of Joseph's disappearance. And these were God's chosen people!

DIAGNOSING THE PAST

To aid in the analysis of your own family system, we suggest you ask yourself the following questions about each nuclear family represented on your genogram:

- ✓ Did this family function in a way consistent with God's plan?
- ✓ Was the father the high priest of the household?
- ✓ Did the parents practice "leave and cleave" with their own families? With their children?
- ✓ What blessing was inherited from the generation before?
- ✓ What has been the heritage of sin? Many such "family sins" exist. A few examples are:

    Spouse abuse
    Child abuse
    Alcohol and drug addiction
    Sexual immorality
    Bad temper; unexplained anger
    Not resolving conflicts
    Failing to communicate
    Being withdrawn from family relationships and activities
    Absentee father or mother
    Keeping family secrets

- ✓ Who actually raised the children?
- ✓ Was parenting shared between Mom and Dad?
- ✓ Was one parent particularly distant?
- ✓ How healthy was this family system?

√ Did your ancestors demonstrate parenting styles that you wish to emulate in your own family?

√ Is there a "black sheep" or incompetent family member in every generation?

√ Are women particularly helpless or men particularly worthless from generation to generation?

CLEANING UP THE PAST

Did you discover any leftovers or significant "anniversary" events as you studied your genogram? Leftovers often prove difficult to identify for a reason that is easy to understand: What do people usually do with leftovers from dinner? They seal them in plastic containers and stick them in the refrigerator. Sometimes they get shoved to the back, maybe for weeks, and when you find them and remove the lid, what's left is a greenish substance of unknown origin.

The same problem exists with emotional leftovers. People like to believe that they can safely push problems and feelings aside and not deal with them. But they don't go away; they sit there taking up space and after a while they become indiscernible masses of emotional garbage. The longer we let them sit, the harder they are to recognize.

However, if we want to make positive changes in our lives and in our families, it becomes very important to recognize them—at least for what they have become. Then we can take action to rid ourselves of them. How?

1. *Inventory your leftover issues.*
   √ Identify them as clearly as possible.
   √ What do you think and feel about each issue?
   √ What triggers the same thoughts and feelings in your present circumstances?

2. *Decide what you wish to change.*
   √ Which of these changes are under your control?
   √ How will these changes involve other family members?

3. *Establish goals to accomplish the changes.*
   √ Set both short-term and long-term goals.
   √ Be sure your goals are measurable.

√ How will you know when each goal is accomplished?

If all this proves too difficult to do alone, seek some godly counseling from a qualified family therapist. The appendix lists referral centers.

FORGIVING THE PAST

As we recognize the sins of our fathers and the leftovers we have from our childhood, the need for forgiveness becomes apparent. God promises that "if we confess our sins, He is faithful and just and will forgive us our sins and purify us from all unrighteousness" (1 John 1:9). Verses such as Matthew 6:14-15 and Mark 11:25 make it clear that we are to extend the same forgiveness to others as God extends to us.

Christ demonstrated two kinds of forgiveness toward men. First, He taught that forgiveness comes through confession and repentance. However, those who sin against us, including parents, aren't always aware of their sin; they may not even be alive for us to talk to about our grievances. In such a situation, Christ showed us another kind of forgiveness—forgiveness because of ignorance. "Jesus said, 'Father, forgive them, for they do not know what they are doing" (Luke 23:34). Forgiveness of others is a necessary step if we are to gain freedom from the past.

Beware of too-hasty forgiveness. Before true forgiveness can take place, you must first allow yourself to experience the pain and grief of those leftover issues. Otherwise, you may find that your emotions stay locked inside you as you continually go over and over the same issues from your past. Refusing to face painful emotions keeps us trapped in the past; going through the pain frees us from it.

THE PAST AS A CLASSROOM

Our family of origin is our first classroom; this is where we receive our education about roles and rules, about limits and boundaries, about values and beliefs. This is where we learn about relationships and what we want and do not want in a mate.

Families, both healthy and unhealthy ones, operate with a

variety of structures and rules. Some are close, some are distant; some have stringent limits, others seemingly none at all. What did you learn about "family" from your family of origin? To find out, let's look through the bottom lens of our bifocals and see if we can draw a more detailed picture of the family in which you grew up.

MEASURING THE FAMILY CIRCLE

The facts you learned about your family while completing your genogram help explain who you are and why you have certain characteristics. The *circumplex,* developed by Dr. David Olson, gives even more insight into your family system and how it influenced your choice of a mate, your expectations of marriage, and your parenting style. This simple tool measures the emotional closeness of your family of origin and the ability of the family to cope with change.

TARGETING FAMILY STYLES

The circumplex resembles a bullseye, with two circles of graduated sizes. Two straight lines divide the circles—the vertical line represents the *adaptability* scale and the horizontal line represents the *cohesion* scale. These lines divide the circle into four quadrants [see figure 8].

The *adaptability* scale examines how the family manages change and decision-making. It looks at how often members perform the same roles in the family; how they solve problems; the type and consistency of discipline; how well the family defines rules; and the amount of change allowed during the family life cycle. Adaptability is measured on a continuum with extreme *chaos* at one end and extreme *rigidity* at the other.

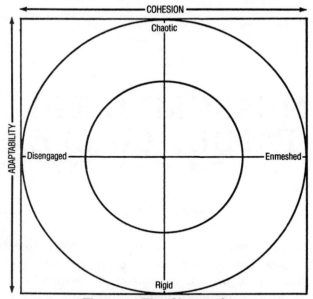

Figure 8. The Circumplex

Chaotic families have no consistent leadership, frequent and dramatic role shifts, erratic discipline, and rapid change. They often fail to clarify roles and seldom enforce their poorly defined rules. Various members assume the task of parenting at different times, but the job passes around so much that no real parental authority exists. Anything goes, and each family member suffers from a lack of sensible guidelines. Some chaotic families do much talking and arguing. Yet, since they take little, if any, action, problems seldom get solved; they're just talked to death.

Rigid families have authoritarian leadership, roles that seldom change, strict discipline, and lack the flexibility necessary to cope with change. This type of family has no problem with defining rules and imposing consequences, but these often fail to be appropriate to the needs of the child or the seriousness of the misdeed. High expectations, unchangeable goals, and harsh punishment mark rigid families to varying degrees. Compliance with rules occurs more out of fear than out of love and a desire to honor parents or spouses.

The *cohesion* scale measures the degree of involvement family members have with each other. It looks at such matters as the amount of loyalty expected of family members, the amount of influence tolerated from outsiders, and the amount of dependence between members. Cohesion is measured on a continuum from extreme *disengagement*, with little interaction between members, to extreme *enmeshment*, with a high, smothering level of closeness.

Those from *disengaged* families show a lack of family loyalty, high independence in making decisions, and little involvement with other family members. Some disengaged families tend to ignore problems, seldom discussing them with each other. "Family business" remains unfinished. In other families, arguing may be a way of life, but they have trouble resolving the arguments. Feelings usually heal quickly, however, because family members allow each other emotional space and privacy. Often, one parent is missing in disengaged families either through divorce, desertion, or failure to function in the role of a parent. This leaves a child with no role model at all for that parent. Work, peer groups, sports, church activities — even gang membership — can become substitutes for the intimacy lacking in these families.

Enmeshed families share a high degree of loyalty to family and are overly dependent on each other. Those from enmeshed families often involve themselves in every decision concerning other family members. Everyone minds everyone else's business. After arguments, which may happen frequently, members tend to nurse hurt feelings longer than those from disengaged families. The need to honor the family name lays the burden of the entire family on each member's shoulders and loyalty smothers individuality.

The closer a family style is to the center of the circumplex, the more *balanced* the family. By balanced we mean that the family has clear, flexible roles and well-defined rules. The family acts for the well-being of its members through emotional support, effective communication, and sensitivity to one another, yet members retain the freedom to pursue individual interests.

Some families function well on one scale of the circumplex, but experience considerable difficulty on the other. For instance, we see families who maintain balance on the cohesion scale, but may suffer from extreme chaos on the adaptability scale. They find it difficult to make decisions and come to a plan of action. On the other hand, some families with clearly defined rules (balanced adaptability) don't allow each other the space and privacy to grow and change as individuals. They function within the enmeshed extreme on the cohesion scale.

Well-functioning families often find that they move from a more structured, involved style to being looser and less involved as the children grow. If a family moves too far out on either or both of the scales, it tends to display symptoms of *dysfunction*. These symptoms can include emotional problems such as depression, anxiety, school performance problems, and eating and behavior disorders. Dysfunctional extremes also can contribute to physical ailments such as migraine headaches, stomach ulcers, and chemical dependency.

Perhaps we can best illustrate the use of the circumplex by looking at some families who display the extremes on both scales. Then we'll analyze their styles and see where they would fall on the circumplex model.

DYSFUNCTIONAL STYLES

Let's look in on four families who live on a cul-de-sac in an average town much like yours. Because of an unusually effective neighborhood canvassing and evangelistic outreach, all four families attend the same church—though not with the same degree of commitment, as we shall see. This particular Sunday, all four have plans to attend church for the annual children's musical program. At least, some of them have plans. . . .

Family number one neglected to set the alarm. The youngest daughter, a participant in today's program, takes it upon herself to rouse the rest of the family in time to dress for church. While the others grumble and search for suitable clothes to wear, she prepares her breakfast and hopes her mother will have time to press the robe she is to wear in the program. The thought of appearing in a wrinkled robe adds to the nervousness in her stomach. Secretly, she wishes her mom and dad would pay more attention to her and what she feels and thinks. The family (except the oldest son who opts to sleep in) leaves for church in shifts, taking two cars, one of which detours toward the local doughnut shop. Eventually, they all arrive at the church and straggle to the only seats left—down front. This family represents a *chaotic disengaged* style.

As the appointed time of departure approaches, family number two begins to gather from various parts of the house. The two sons sullenly await their father's judgment on their choice of clothing, and their performance of the morning's mandatory chores. When Dad reaches for his Bible the youngest boy risks a glance at his older brother, rolling his eyes upward in disgust. Once, in a fit of anger, the older boy confided in his brother that he was "getting out of here" when he turned 18 and was never coming back. The boys occupy their assigned seats on the drive to church and silently daydream as Mom reminds her youngest son that she expects him to behave himself during the program. As soon as the car stops, both boys are off in their own directions, generally causing havoc and misbehaving at every opportunity. The parents make their way to their usual pew, never giving their children another thought. Out of sight, out of mind, and a strict adherence to the rules when in sight, describes their approach to parenting. This style is both *rigid* and *disengaged.*

In some ways, family number three looks very much like our first family—clothes unready and milk missing from the breakfast table. No one knows who to blame for this (because no one knows who's responsible for anything) so they spend valuable time blaming each other. This family seems to thrive on conflict, with each member taking personal interest in the way the others dress and how they behave in public. Each firmly believes that what one family member does reflects on all the others. They manage to get ready in spite of the chaos and arrive at church only a few minutes late. Mother rushes the youngest into the restroom to finish grooming her for the program, taking one last opportunity to rehearse the all-too-familiar lines. She could never bear the embarrassment of her child forgetting her part. *Chaotic enmeshment* is the style of family three.

Family number four enters the sanctuary several minutes before the start of the program and begins greeting others as they make their way to their usual spot. Each member, dressed neatly and appropriately, smiles and nods to acquaintances and strangers alike. Others marvel at the togetherness displayed by family four, somehow feeling that this family serves as a model for all the others in the church. But the inner turmoil of each family member doesn't show. The tension involved in trying to please everyone in the family smothers the individuality of each family member. Mother chooses the clothing that each wears; father dictates the Sunday morning schedule with no deviation allowed. As in family two, this family tolerates no questioning of father's demands; as in family three, each member feels acutely attached to the others and privacy doesn't exist. In family four, the family itself matters more than any of the individual members. This family demonstrates a *rigid enmeshed* style.

CHARTING THE STYLES

Each of these families reveals either a closeness that smothers individuality, or an indifference that denies the very idea of family. They show flexibility that ranges from no structure at all to a conformity that rejects the need for growth and change. Each displays a style out of balance on both scales of the circumplex, a common situation for families. Now let's plot these families on the circumplex and see if we can better define the emotional climate within the families and the strengths and weaknesses of each system.

Look back at family one. No one member of the family is the leader; each takes care of his or her own needs. Individuals make decisions about participating in family events, claiming ownership of their feelings with no responsibility to any other family member. How "I" feel reigns. Family one is flexible to the point of *chaos* and *disengaged* from each other.

After measuring the cohesion and adaptability of the family, we'll place family one on the outer circle of the upper left quadrant of the circumplex, indicated by an X [see figure 9].

Now look back at family two—no doubt about who makes the decisions in this family. Father, the unquestioned but not necessarily respected leader, spells out the rules and hands them down to be obeyed without discussion. This family has no problem with chaos! Still, communication between members doesn't take place and family two appears no closer emotionally than family one. We'll place them in the lower left quadrant, showing the family's *rigidly disengaged* style [see figure 9].

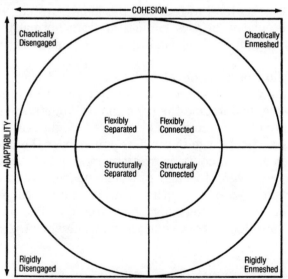

Figure 9. The Circumplex Showing Types of Dysfunctional Families

Family three shows some characteristics of the first family. Chaos and lack of structure govern their lives. Yet, they differ from families one and two by displaying a lack of emotional boundary lines between members. How "we" feel replaces how "I" feel, with the family sharing ownership of feelings.

Because of this, each person becomes overinvolved in the lives of the others; what one feels they all feel. Family three belongs in the upper right quadrant of the circumplex, again on the outer circle, showing the extreme *chaotic enmeshment* of the family style [see figure 9].

The last family shows the extreme rigidity of family two with the overinvolvement of family three. Family members have decisions made for them, family loyalty is important above all other matters, and each member "feels" and thinks for the others. This *rigidly enmeshed* family falls in the lower right quadrant [see figure 9].

Most families fall somewhere between these extremes. You may recognize some characteristics of your family of origin as you study the four families we described. Like it or not, most of us tend to recreate the family system we came out of because what *feels* familiar appears normal to us. As you may already realize, familiar does not necessarily mean healthy.

The following test, developed by Dr. David Olson, professor of family social science at the University of Minnesota, will help you understand the cohesion or "togetherness," and adaptability of your family of origin. You might find it helpful to have a particular age in mind as you answer the questions. Choose an age that contains many memories for you, or think of when you were the age of your children. Answer each question for yourself — other family members probably remember things differently than you do. The important thing to look for is how your parents influenced *you*.

FAMILY ADAPTABILITY

Circle the number that you feel best describes your family.
1. What kind of leadership was there in your family?

1	2	3	4
one person usually led	leadership often was shared	leadership sometimes was shared	no clear leader

2. How often did family members do the same things (roles) around the house?

1	2	3	4
always did the same things	often did the same things	sometimes did the same things	seldom did the same things

3. What were the rules (written or unwritten) like in your family?

1	2	3	4
rules very clear and very stable	rules clear and stable	rules clear and flexible	rules seldom clear and changed often

4. How was discipline of children handled?

1	2	3	4
very strict	democratic and predictable	democratic but unpredictable	very lenient

5. How effective was the family at solving problems?

1	2	3	4
extremely effective	usually effective	sometimes effective	seldom effective

FAMILY ADAPTABILITY SCORE _____
(sum x 5)

FAMILY TOGETHERNESS

1. How close did you feel to other family members?

1	2	3	4
not very close	moderately close	very close	extremely close

2. How often did your family spend time playing together?

1	2	3	4
seldom	sometimes	often	very often

3. How often did individuals make their own decisions?

1	2	3	4
each family member usually made his/her own decisions	each family member often made his/her own decisions	each family member seldom made his/her own decisions	each family member rarely made his/her own decisions

4. How independent or dependent were family members?

1	2	3	4
independent	somewhat independent	usually dependent	very dependent

5. Answer either part a or b.

a. For married couples—

How close were the husband and wife?

1	2	3	4
seldom close	moderately close	very close	extremely close

b. For single parent families—

How close was the parent to another adult?

1	2	3	4
seldom close	moderately close	very close	extremely close

FAMILY TOGETHERNESS SCORE _____
(sum x 5)

[See figure 10 for scoring.]

UNDERSTANDING THE RESULTS

Each dysfunctional family type determined by the circumplex carries its own set of problems and its own unique set of solutions. The circumplex allows us to see where the family structure or relationship breaks down and in which direction you must move to restore balance. Parents in dysfunctional families may well be adult children of dysfunctional families themselves, and the danger exists that they will pass the

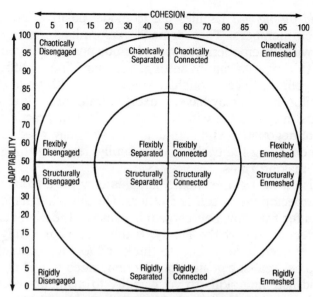

Figure 10. Circumplex for Scoring Test

dysfunctional behavior of the family on to their children. This is the pattern of Exodus 34:7, discussed in chapter 1.

If you grew up in a *chaotic disengaged,* family you may find that you lack the ability to identify relationship issues before they turn to problems. It may be difficult to relate to the feelings of others in your family. You also may lack understanding of the various roles of the family or how to set and maintain consistent goals. Adequate problem-solving skills can help in each of these areas.

If you came from a *chaotic enmeshed* family, you may find it easy to take responsibility for everyone but yourself. You must first learn to think and feel for yourself and to allow others that same freedom. You also may need to learn to take steps to resolve problems after discussing them. This requires learning to detach yourself from the emotions of an issue and to look at problems more objectively. Like the person from a chaotic disengaged family, you must learn to spell out and consistently apply appropriate roles and consequences.

Rigid disengaged families fail to model positive interaction between members. They demand conformity to family standards without emotional support for one another. If you grew up in this type of family setting, you may find it difficult to share your feelings, thoughts, and desires with your spouse and children. You may have to exert extra effort in learning to be sensitive to others in your family, and in practicing the skills of negotiating and listening. You also may need to adapt to the changing life cycle of your family, learning to be flexible in making rules.

Those from *rigid enmeshed* families may have trouble with high expectations of self and others. On the other hand, they may suffer from low self-esteem because of the high standard of perfection set by the family. If this was your family type, you may need to learn how to think and feel for yourself, and how to set realistic goals. You also may need to add negotiating and listening skills to your ability to maintain discipline.

Each family style discussed lacks adequate problem-solving skills. In chapter 5, we will discuss the process of problem solving and conflict resolution.

THE BLAME GAME

Now that we have analyzed and categorized your family of origin, let's stop and talk about what this means. Too few of us discover a balanced and well-structured family of origin. Don't be distressed if your family was dysfunctional; most are out of balance to some degree. You can break free from the negative lessons of the past and with a little fine tuning your nuclear family can become a smooth-functioning one.

Some of you may discover disturbing leftovers from your growing-up years. You may begin to feel that your parents made mistakes and now you must pay for them. The temptation to blame can cloud the mind, making it impossible to see beyond the hurts of an abusive or abandoned childhood. God never gives us the right to heap revenge and guilt on parents and siblings, and He never condones self-pity. Instead, as He promises in Romans 8:28, He will in all things work "for the good of those who love Him."

Even those things that others do to harm us can be turned to good for us. Joseph had his share of sibling rivalry and suffered much at the hands of his brothers. Yet he modeled the proper attitude for us in Genesis 50:20: "You intended to harm me, but God intended it for good to accomplish what is now being done, the saving of many lives."

In chapter 1 we stated that we can be victims of our families or we can profit from them. We must choose which way we will view our childhood. James 1:2-4 and Romans 5:3-5 both state that God uses trials and suffering to develop godly character in our lives. In truth, most of our parents were doing the best they could with the knowledge and skills they possessed, just as we attempt to do with our own children.

The time comes when, as adults, we must decide to take responsibility for our own actions and stop blaming the past for making us the way we are. Then we can choose to examine the past to discover what needs to change in our own lives. By making these changes, we will become better partners in our marriages and better parents to our children. If you find yourself wanting to blame your parents for their mistakes, instead of taking action to correct your own, try rereading the section "Forgiving the Past" in chapter 2.

FROM THE PAST INTO THE PRESENT

Now it's time to shift our focus from the past to the present and look at the results our family-born beliefs and attitudes produce in our marriages and families. Take the self-test again, this time grading your nuclear family. As you plot your results on the circumplex, be alert for similarities between your family of origin and your nuclear family. Which of your family system's traits did you bring into your marriage? Will these characteristics help the following generations become godly partners and parents? If not, keep reading. There is much more to learn about family systems.

CHECKING THE FOUNDATION

It has been our experience that parents often come to a family therapist asking the wrong questions. We find that we can't give parents techniques for making children mind when the marriage isn't working. Sometimes, one parent in a malfunctioning marriage finds himself or herself forced into operating like a single parent. Chapter 9, "The Absent Parent," may offer some help if you find yourself in this type of situation.

In any family system there exists a variety of smaller systems—*subsystems*—that consist of two people who share a relationship. The first of these subsystems, the husband and wife, forms the foundation of the nuclear family. Even before Adam and Eve became parents, God proclaimed that marriage was the reason that "a man will leave his father and mother and be united to his wife, and they will become one flesh" (Genesis 2:24). Getting unstuck from our families of origin must happen before we can successfully become glued to our partner in marriage. For some, this may mean violating a long tradition of "stuckness"; others may find their glue has dried out from disuse.

CHAPTER FOUR

FIRST THINGS FIRST

She resents cleaning up the hair in the bathroom. It makes her feel like her husband's servant. He can't understand why she never seems to get the laundry folded and put away. He hates digging through a basket for underwear and socks. His driving drives her right up the wall, and her constant chatter sends him in search of a quiet corner and a newspaper.

Does the marriage exist that escapes such day-to-day annoyances as these? In the face of adulterous affairs, abuse, and abandonment, matters such as unfolded underwear and hair in the bathroom sink seem trivial. Yet, trivial matters may hide much deeper issues—issues that can lead to the breakdown and eventual breakup of an apparently stable marriage.

This chapter explores some necessary ingredients for a satisfying and rewarding marriage. The next chapter takes a closer look at common marriage problems and offers some suggestions for improving the vital marriage subsystem. It may seem odd in a parenting book to spend so much time looking at marriage. We are convinced, however, that the best thing you can do in parenting is to present your children with a stable marriage. Because of this, we believe that these next two chapters may be the most important in this entire book.

A host of problem behaviors and emotional symptoms in children result from the lack of a secure marriage subsystem. When parents fail to agree on parenting issues, or undermine the authority of one another, the children often become insecure, nervous, frustrated, or angry. In some cases, a child may decide to do as he pleases because the parents can't get their act together and offer consistent discipline and guidance.

Children can and will grow up—physically—in any environment; that process cannot be stopped. But if a husband and wife want to rear well-adjusted children who will carry a minimum of emotional leftovers into their adulthood, they must provide a solid and secure foundation for the family.

PUTTING YOUR HOUSE IN ORDER

Matthew 6:33 tells us to "seek first [God's] kingdom and His righteousness." We put God first by loving Him, honoring Him and obeying His commands, or as Psalm 119:9 states, "by living according to [God's] Word." This includes taking to heart all God's instructions to husbands and wives. Many scriptural principles apply to the marriage relationship. Three seem closely related to our discussion of the family as a system.

Genesis 2:24 gives the first of these instructions: "For this cause a man shall leave his father and mother, and shall cleave to his wife; and they shall become one flesh" (NASB). This verse tells us to leave the childlike emotional dependence on our family of origin and to join emotionally and physically to our new mate, putting him/her above all others. In our language the word *cleave* carries with it the connotation of severing or cutting away and also gluing or sticking together. To connect with your mate, you must first experience a certain amount of detachment from your family of origin.

I AM THE HEAD . . . YOU ARE THE FEET

Next to leaving and cleaving, the question of leadership and submission in a marriage may be the most crucial—and the most often misunderstood. Ephesians 5:21-33 and 1 Peter 3:1-7 teach that wives are to "submit to your husbands *as to the Lord.*" Husbands are to "love your wives just *as Christ loves the church*" (emphases added), laying down their lives and treating their wives as "heirs with you of the gracious gift of life."

In both submission and leadership, Christ provides a living example for men and women to follow. Philippians 2:5-8, a beautiful picture of Christ's submission, tells us that "your attitude should be the kind that was shown us by Jesus Christ, who, though He was God, did not demand and cling to His rights as God, but laid aside His mighty power and glory, taking the disguise of a slave and becoming like men" (TLB). John 13:1-17 tells the story of Christ washing the disciples' feet, a true demonstration of humility and submission. Christ adapted Himself to the needs of those He served. Throughout His life on earth, Christ showed us that submission does not lie solely in the woman's domain. As Paul instructs us in Ephesians 5:21, men and women alike should "submit to one another out of reverence for Christ."

As a leader, Christ showed humility and compassion. He led by example, setting people free from bondage, never demanding or controlling, and motivating through love. He lived with the attitude of forgiveness spoken of in 1 Corinthians 13:5: "[Love] . . . keeps no record of wrongs." He gave His life for the very ones who rejected Him.

Scripture also gives us pictures of women who showed characteristics of leadership. For example, Mary, the mother of Jesus, displayed unusual strength and independence in at least two instances. The first occurred when she chose to go to Jerusalem to visit Elizabeth. The second happened when she decided to accompany Joseph to Bethlehem for the birth of her child. To use circumplex terms to describe Mary's actions, she was not enmeshed with Joseph or rigidly under his control. Instead, she exercised freedom of judgment and independent thinking.

The "wife of noble character" described in Proverbs 31 also lends insight into a woman of independent character. She "considers a field and buys it" and "plants a vineyard." She "sees that her trading is profitable" and "makes linen garments and sells them, and supplies the merchants with sashes." Even with all this individual activity, "her children . . . call her blessed; her husband also, and he praises her." We should not twist submission to mean that a wife's role is just to care for the children and follow her husband's orders. The uniqueness of marriage allows leadership and submission to characterize the roles of both the husband and the wife.

Just as Christ serves as our example in leadership and submission, the Trinity provides a picture of marriage structure. No hierarchy exists in the Godhead; instead, Father, Son, and Holy Spirit share a diversity of roles in the salvation and life of believers. They are equal; They are one; They are God. Marriage also carries no hierarchy, simply a difference in the roles of husband and wife; roles do not denote status, merely responsibility.

The responsibilities of husbands and wives spelled out by Scripture clearly suggest that attitude plays a more significant part in a successful marriage than fulfilling specific duties. God created wives to help their husbands and to fit in with their husband's plans (Genesis 2:18). In addition to being "busy at home" and loving her children, a wife is to respect her husband and be kind (Titus 2:4-5). She should conduct her life with purity and modesty, not giving way to fear (1 Peter 3:2-6), and she should "bring [her husband] good, not harm, all the days of her life" (Proverbs 31:12).

Husbands don't get off lightly either. Scripture teaches that they are to "love [their] wives, just as Christ loved the church, and gave Himself up for her" (Ephesians 5:25). They are not only to sacrifice themselves for their wives, but they must also provide for their families (1 Timothy 5:8). First Peter 3:7 instructs husbands to "be considerate as you live with your wives and treat them with respect." What does it mean to be considerate? Thoughtful, attentive, generous, tender, warm, affectionate, gentle, responsive, and sympathetic are a few synonyms that give us a glimpse of the meaning behind God's guidelines for husbands.

MUTUALLY SATISFYING

First Corinthians 7:5 offers some interesting instructions to a husband and wife: "Do not deprive each other *except by mutual consent* and for a time, so that you may devote yourselves to prayer" (emphasis added). This verse speaks specifically to the sexual union in marriage, but it also gives us the only picture in Scripture of a husband and wife resolving an issue. They discussed the matter and agreed on a course of action. The verse does not suggest an enmeshed relationship — thinking the same thoughts or feeling the same feelings. Instead, it implies consideration and tolerance for differences, and a willingness to work together toward a mutual goal.

As we saw in our discussion of the circumplex in chapter 3, chaotic families either do no talking, or talk to the point of distraction with no follow-through. In either case, decisions are hard to come by. In rigid families, decisions come down from the self-appointed leader with no discussion allowed. However, much silent dissension may take place among the remaining family members. In a healthy marriage, partners make decisions jointly, talking the matter out and allowing for differences of feelings and opinions. They then come to a mutual agreement on the action to take; one partner does not impose his or her will on the other.

As Pastor Tim Timmons used to stress in the Christian Family Life Seminars, marriage is not a 50/50 proposition; it is 100/100, with each partner giving and giving and giving some more. What matters to one partner in the marriage matters to the other because each values the feelings and opinions of his or her spouse. Both partners must willingly sacrifice selfish desires to maintain balance in the marriage.

God's design for marriage, therefore, includes: separating emotionally from both families of origin; putting your spouse above all others; properly carrying out the roles of the relationship with humility and gentleness; and working to resolve issues in a way that is agreeable to both husband and wife. Practicing these steps helps build a strong marriage unit and enables you to model for your children healthy characteristics that they will carry with them into their own marriages.

MARRIAGE MYTHS

Marriages sometimes get sidetracked from scriptural priorities when children enter the picture and the family begins to change. Children often occupy a place in the family that rightly belongs to a mate, and a "child-focused marriage" develops. When this happens, husbands and wives fail to model the scriptural principles that children need to see. Staying together for the sake of the children, staying married because it is your Christian duty, and living for your children suggest that marriage priorities are out of balance. Each of these myths involves holding the marriage together for the wrong reasons.

Staying together for the sake of the children violates the first scriptural principle we discussed in this chapter—obeying God by putting your partner first. It also makes the children responsible for the marriage, a responsibility that God never intended for children to carry. Our rule of thumb for our clients is simple but often shocking: *You must value your marriage more than your role as a parent.* Before you begin to protest, read the second part of the rule: Take the value you place on your role of being a parent and don't touch it. Keep it as high as you have established it—but then place the importance of your marriage one notch above that. We violate this principle when we side with our children against our mate, or undermine our mate's authority as a parent.

Staying together because it is your Christian duty fails to honor God because of failing to honor your mate. As we noted above, 1 Peter 3:1-7 outlines the need for husbands to respect their wives "so that nothing will hinder your prayers." Proverbs 31:12 tells wives to do good to their husbands. Our Christian duty calls us to obey these commands, searching for new and creative ways to fulfill our role in the marriage. Bitterness often sets in and blame-shifting occurs when one partner begins to think, "I'm stuck in this miserable marriage because my mate isn't what he or she should be." This attitude often hides a blindness to one's own mistakes in the relationship, and an unwillingness to take responsibility for one's own actions and attitudes. Nothing so hides us from ourselves as playing the part of a martyr.

Living for your children fails both your children and your marriage. More than anything else, children need to observe a mother and a father who love each other and truly work at strengthening their relationship. To do this, you must pour your energy into your marriage as well as into your children. We can't say it often enough: *Children need their parents to have a healthy marriage.*

GROWING STRONG IN WEDDED LIFE

To create a vital, growing marriage, a husband and wife need time together without children, friends, or other family members. Doing things together that both enjoy, be it taking a long walk or listening to music, often leads to times of sharing deep feelings and thoughts. The committed husband and wife make it a priority to get to know each other on a deeper level.

A good marriage needs open and frequent expression of affection. Love requires both words and actions. It is not enough to declare your love on your wedding day and assume that your partner still feels that love 30 years later just because you haven't revoked it.

Couples also need to communicate affirmation and approval for each other and their roles in the family. Daily encouragement offers hope and promotes growth and positive change not only in the marriage relationship but in each partner's personal life as well.

Shared religious experiences and growing together spiritually add an important dimension to a healthy marriage. What if you, a Christian, are married to a nonbeliever? Look at how Jesus handled His relationships with nonbelievers. He met them where they were, welcoming sinners and eating with them (Luke 15:2). He shared Himself with them, meeting their physical and emotional needs (Matthew 8:16). He showed them respect and understanding (Mark 1:40-41), and never hounded them or belittled them because of the state of their souls (John 8:1-11). We would do well to follow His example, while maintaining a readiness to explain our beliefs in a rational, non-condemning way (1 Peter 3:15).

A similar word of caution applies to those married to believers who don't appear concerned with Bible study and personal spiritual growth. This situation again calls for a spirit of understanding and acceptance, allowing your partner room for personal differences in the rate of learning and growth. If your partner does not seem interested at all in spiritual matters, prayer on his or her behalf seems the wisest course of action.

BUILDING ON BEDROCK

If you want to build a strong marriage based on the wisdom of God's Word, heed the words of Matthew 7:24: "Therefore everyone who hears these words of Mine and puts them into practice is like a wise man who built his house on the rock." At least two commitments are necessary at this stage if you want to lay a solid, unshakable foundation on which to build your family system. The first involves making a firm commitment to Christ and to following the scriptural principles for marriage, including the ones we shared earlier in this chapter.

God designed marriage; no one knows better than He how to make it work. Don't take this commitment lightly, however. Jesus warned the crowds who followed Him to count the cost of discipleship (Luke 14:25-35). When you count, include His promises in Philippians 2:13 and Hebrews 13:5 — He not only helps us do His will, but helps us want to do it, and He never leaves us or forsakes us. No one else can offer you a deal like that.

The second necessity for laying a solid foundation involves making a commitment to your mate. Adam set the example for us when he, without restraint, accepted Eve as God's gift to him. When I see my mate as God's provision for me, I no longer question the rightness of my marriage.

This acceptance of my mate brings two results. First, if my mate is a gift from God to me, and I commit to following His principles for marriage, then I must find a way to work out my differences with my mate. Divorce ceases to be an option.

In our years of family practice, we have observed that it takes the same relationship skills to be successfully divorced as it takes to be successfully married, especially if there are children involved. Why not apply all that energy to improving your marriage instead of your divorce?

Receiving my mate as a gift from God also puts an end to making comparisons between my mate and someone else. Comparisons are deadly; few mates can live up to the idealized vision of someone we've never had to live with. Second Corinthians 10:12 says, "When they measure themselves by themselves and compare themselves with themselves, they are not wise." Instead of spending valuable mental energy in making comparisons, use your mind to study your mate. Learn all you can about your partner's unique personality, likes, dislikes, and interests. If you have trouble treating your mate in a respectful way because of differences in personality or the flaws you see, you may need to seek help. Often, someone with a more objective viewpoint can assist you in learning to use creative, imaginative ways to meet your mate's needs.

ANALYZING THE SUBSYSTEM

Use the following self-test, also developed by Dr. David Olson, to analyze your marriage relationship on the circumplex. This test seeks to help you think of your marriage in terms of family systems and does not address areas such as marital satisfaction or sexual intimacy. Think only of how you and your spouse relate without the children or anyone else present.

MARITAL ADAPTABILITY

1. What kind of leadership is there in your marriage?

1	2	3	4
one person usually leads	leadership is sometimes shared	leadership is often shared	no clear leader

2. How often do you and your partner change or switch chores around the house?

1	2	3	4
seldom change chores	sometimes change chores	often change chores	very often change chores

3. What are the rules like in your marriage?

1	2	3	4
rules very clear and very stable	rules clear and stable	rules clear and flexible	rules unclear and/or change often

4. How much has your marriage changed over time?

1	2	3	4
very little change	some change	much change	very much change

5. How do you and your partner settle disagreements?

1	2	3	4
little discussion, one person decides	some discussion, one person decides	some discussion, both decide	much discussion, no clear decision

MARITAL ADAPTABILITY SCORE ＿＿＿＿＿
(sum x 5)

MARITAL TOGETHERNESS

1. How close do you feel to your partner?

1	2	3	4
seldom close	generally close	very close	extremely close

2. How often do you and your partner make your own decisions?

1	2	3	4
always	very often	often	sometimes

3. How often do you and your partner spend time having fun together?

1	2	3	4
seldom	sometimes	often	very often

4. How often do you depend on each other?

1	2	3	4
seldom	sometimes	often	very often

5. How often do you and your partner do things together?

1	2	3	4
seldom	sometimes	often	very often

MARITAL TOGETHERNESS SCORE _____
(sum x 5)

[See figure 11 for scoring.]

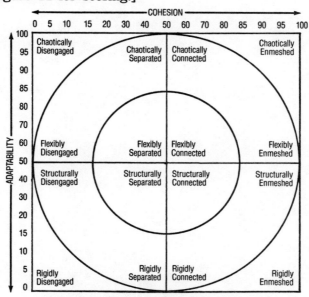

Figure 11. Circumplex for Scoring Test

CONSIDER THE OPTIONS

Chapter 5 explores the results of the self-test and delves further into this all-important subsystem by looking at some common problems that arise in marriage. It then presents some ideas for strengthening your marriage partnership, while at the same time improving your effectiveness as a parent.

CHAPTER FIVE

Rx FOR CHANGE

Millie kicked off her shoes, tossed her purse onto the counter, picked up the telephone, and blew a quick kiss in the direction of her husband. Lance smiled halfheartedly and tried not to show his irritation with her nightly call to her mother.

Millie's constant dependence on her mother for approval and advice went against his desire to meet his new bride's needs. When Lance finally worked up the courage to speak to Millie about his feelings, he discovered Millie didn't know that her phone calls home bothered him.

Owen and Cathy had been married for just over a year when Owen's father died and Owen invited his mother to live with them. Cathy tried to share her concern over the arrangement but Owen never seemed to hear what she said. From the day they returned from their honeymoon, Cathy had quietly suffered the intrusions of her mother-in-law. She constantly criticized Cathy for everything, from the way she peeled potatoes to the way she made the bed. Now, escape appeared impossible. She had no voice in family affairs and quickly began to feel more like a hired servant than a wife.

Improper launching from families of origin threatened both of these marriages. Those from smothering, enmeshed families, such as Millie, often have trouble leaving their familiar nest to create a new family unit. Emotions remain tied to parents and siblings though physical separation takes place. Disengaged families tend to produce members who, never having witnessed true intimacy in their parents' marriage, find they have difficulty connecting, or cleaving, to their new marriage partner. This was the case with Owen and Cathy.

The principle of leaving and cleaving applies whether or not you come from a family system that encourages it. You must take the necessary steps to let your partner know in tangible ways that you honor and esteem him/her above all others. You can do this by valuing your partner's feelings and opinions. Make time for your partner away from the demands of others, and strive for financial independence from both families. Parents can aid in the "leaving and cleaving" process by encouraging their married children to look to their spouses for support and counsel.

Leaving your family does not mean that you cannot ask for advice when you and your partner have a difficult decision to make. When you married, however, your parents' role changed from *supervisor* to *consultant.* Supervisors oversee the work and choices of others; consultants do not take responsibility for the decisions made by those who ask for advice. You and your partner are free to seek counsel from your parents, and you can choose either to take their advice or ignore it. But you can't ignore your partner's desires. Ultimately, the final decision must be made by you and your partner and it must be agreeable to both of you.

EXPECTATIONS AND THE STATUS QUO
Difficulties in marriage can develop for reasons other than not cutting emotional ties. Failure to define the new roles of husband and wife presents many opportunities for misunderstanding. In our first case study mentioned earlier, Millie had one set of expectations for her new husband's role in the family; Lance had a different idea of the role he wanted to fill. Millie's dad lost himself in the newspaper after a busy workday. She seldom saw interaction between her parents. Millie and her mom had established a close friendship during her adolescent years. Now, Millie not only feared abandoning her

mom, but also having to relate in an unfamiliar way to her new mate. Lance's father, on the other hand, took time to listen and actively communicate with his family. Lance wanted the same kind of intimacy with his wife.

Unlike Lance, Owen, the husband in our second case study, grew up in a rigid, disengaged family. He asked his mother to live with him and Cathy after his father's death, not because of emotional attachment to her, but because his mother expected it. Out of habit, he obeyed his mother's commands in the same sullen, withdrawn way his father had. Cathy came from a chaotic, disengaged family with an alcoholic mother. Her father's sole involvement with the family consisted of frequent and abusive arguments with his wife. For Cathy, the safest way to exist in such an environment was to be quiet and nondemanding. When she met Owen, who seemed gentle and unassuming, she thought she had found the answer to her prayers for a peaceful home life.

Unfortunately, Owen's gentleness merely disguised the same type of indifference toward Cathy's family as her father had shown. Because of her lifelong fear of asserting herself, she could not confront Owen openly. Nagging proved useless so she kept quiet, continuing her pattern of suffering in silence. All the while, her bitter spirit grew, along with her resentment of Owen and animosity toward his mother.

Cathy's struggle shows us another problem that often originates from family of origin difficulties. When we seek a mate, our concept of normality can lead us to select someone who has an old familiar "feel." We may, without realizing it, choose to marry someone who helps us continue the problems of the system we desperately wanted to escape from. In this way we persist in our attempts to fix what was wrong in our family of origin. However, if our partner doesn't want "fixing" (and they seldom do), nothing gets solved and the problems get passed on to the next generation.

TESTING THE FOUNDATION
The depth of a couple's marital problems determines the amount of help necessary to bring the marriage into balance.

It's a bit like redoing a house. With a sound foundation and structure, some cosmetic changes may be all a house needs to make it more attractive and efficient. Weak, rotting structures, however, require tearing down and rebuilding before applying a coat of paint or hanging new curtains.

The framework of a marriage also must be tested to decide whether to redecorate or rebuild. Millie and Lance understood the scriptural principles for marriage; they just needed some redecorating: redefining of roles and rearranging of priorities. Owen and Cathy's marriage was structurally unsound from the beginning. For them, ripping out all the misconceptions and wrong beliefs about marriage and family must occur before their relationship can be rebuilt.

THE MEASURE OF A MARRIAGE

If you haven't taken the marriage wellness test in chapter 4, turn back and do so now. Marriages can be out of order on either one or two of the scales of the circumplex, just as the family styles we discussed in chapter 3. Many characteristics of family styles also hold true for the marriage relationship.

A *chaotic disengaged* marriage involves no planning, no common goals, and little companionship. The husband and wife seldom participate in family traditions. What intimacy they have comes and goes, determined by external factors instead of love. Their communication may consist of nothing but small talk, or they may engage in frequent arguments with no resolution of the issue. In effect, the husband and wife live private, parallel lives with no true emotional intimacy. They each have outside interests and activities to fill the void left by a marriage empty of talking, sympathetic listening, or display of affection.

To balance this marriage, and yet stay within the same upper left quadrant of the circumplex, this couple would move toward developing a *flexibly detached* relationship [see figure 12]. This type of marriage allows "breathing room" for both partners to maintain separate, outside interests. Each partner learns, through observation and discussion, to appreciate the uniqueness of the other. They share a sense of fun when together and work at both emotional and physical intimacy, seeking time alone together. Good communication skills allow them to discuss issues before they become problems and to develop action plans and set goals for their marriage.

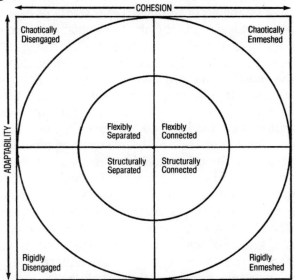

Figure 12. Circumplex Showing Types of Marriage Relationships

In the *rigidly disengaged* marriage, one or both partners lack flexibility, holding firm to attitudes and beliefs detrimental to the marriage. Because no structure for discussion exists, roles and rules, even unhealthy ones, remain permanently in place. Fear of a demanding partner can prevent growth in the marriage. Spiritual development can suffer also, and religion often becomes rule-oriented and legalistic. Physical intimacy may be difficult because of hidden feelings or hostilities; no emotional intimacy exists. Instead of taking the time to understand the partner's feelings, the more demanding partner often attempts to tell the other what he or she "should" think and feel.

To achieve a better balance, the rigid disengaged marriage needs to become more *structured* and *detached* [see figure 12].

This style will still meet the couple's needs for clearly defined yet separate roles.

The roles and expectations agreed on by both partners allow room for necessary growth and change over the course of the marriage. Learning to share feelings and to listen brings understanding of the needs and wants of each partner. This leads to respect and the ability to establish true intimacy without fear. As in the flexibly detached marriage, both partners freely pursue outside interests and friendships.

For the *chaotic enmeshed* marriage, much talk accompanies a lack of clear-cut goals and little, if any, action. This couple's conversations may frequently turn to arguments and one or both partners may tend to sulk for extended periods of time. The need for "oneness" absorbs separate identities. Each partner talks for the other, making the assumption that he or she understands what the other thinks and feels. Because of the enmeshed status of the relationship, little privacy exists and there is low tolerance for outside friends and activities. The husband and wife are too dependent on each other without really knowing why, and each feels hurt if the other doesn't show the same degree of dependence.

To balance this marriage, the couple must move toward becoming *flexibly connected* [see figure 12], allowing space for friends and for personal growth. This style involves more shared activities, projects, and friends than those in detached marriages. Dependence on God and increased self-reliance replace overdependence on each other. True intimacy develops in an atmosphere of love and acceptance of differences.

Rigidly enmeshed relationships add legalistic demands to overdependence. One partner, the authoritarian, demands perfect adherence to his or her definition of the roles and rules of the marriage. This partner may believe that love equals agreement, and that disagreement means rejection. The other partner, perhaps more quiet and meek, can feel stifled by a lack of independence and privacy. The authoritative spouse may belittle and emotionally abuse the more passive mate. In extreme cases, physical abuse may take place. The couple nevertheless keeps up the appearances of a happily married pair. They hold the relationship together at any cost, never allowing the outside world a chance to see the inner workings of the marriage.

To move toward the center of the circumplex, this couple should work at being *structured* and *connected* [see figure 12]. This marriage needs to retain well-defined roles and expectations but add the dimension of unconditional acceptance. The couple will share interests together, yet each partner will be free to build friendships outside the marriage, and to grow and change as individuals.

As you think of your marriage in the light of the previous discussion, list the characteristics of your marriage as they relate to both scales—adaptability and cohesion. Ask yourself the following questions:

√ Is your marriage out of balance on either one or both scales?

√ Which direction(s) do you need to move to establish balance?

√ What characteristics of your marriage do you want to see change?

√ What would your marriage look like if these changes were to take place?

√ What changes do you want your mate to make? What changes are you willing to make?

√ What steps can you begin to take to begin moving toward balance?

UPSETTING THE SYSTEM

By now you should have a pretty good feel for the state of your marriage. May we suggest that you ask yourself another question? What problems face you, what resistance can you expect, as you attempt to bring about a change in your relationship? We must add a word of caution here. *Change upsets the balance of a system.* Because of this, many unhappy couples don't follow through on efforts to correct problems in their marriage or family.

Changes involve risk; you must leave comfort zones behind for new and unfamiliar ways of relating. If you attempt to change your relationship to your spouse, expect some conflict and resistance. The amount of resistance encountered depends on the amount and type of change you attempt to make—and who you try to change. You have little, if any, control over changing your partner. You have maximum control over changing yourself, and you can minimize resistance by concentrating on your own changes first.

Resistance can range from silence to threats, from sulking to physical illness. You may encounter attempts to gain pity or an outright refusal to cooperate. Anticipating resistance allows you to plan for it instead of being surprised by it. Treat resistance with patience, understanding, and a firm resolve to make the change you have initiated. Verbally reaffirm your commitment to your mate and to your marriage.

If your marriage needs sweeping and drastic changes—if you must tear out the foundation of the marriage and rebuild—don't attempt these changes without professional help. Even if your partner sees the need for change and is willing to work on the relationship, you may need outside help. A trained professional can give guidance in new methods of behavior and new ways of relating to each other.

If you have an unwilling partner, we assure you that one person can make a difference in a relationship—but it takes longer and is much harder. A skilled Christian counselor can offer much in the way of support and direction in such situations.

HEARING AIDS

Couples can easily fall into the rut of using ineffective communication styles. For example, spouses may speak in directives that attempt to control and give commands. Turning the blame back on your partner and sending mixed messages—saying one thing and implying another—frequently cause communication breakdown. Arguing can become a habitual form of conversation. Other styles include being over-responsible by speaking for your partner, or being under-responsible and speaking for no one—not even yourself.

Poor listening skills present other problems. The ability to listen requires mental effort and the willingness to put off thinking about what you want to say next. Listening skills include making sure you understand exactly what the other person is saying. Misunderstandings occur daily in conversation because words carry very different connotations to individuals. A person's history colors understanding of, and emotional reactions to, the words he or she hears.

Clear, straightforward communication is difficult but attainable for both adults and children. Chapter 13 discusses steps to effective communication for the entire family. The following discussion on problem solving lays the groundwork for an attitude of valuing your partner, an underlying principle of good communication.

SOLVING PROBLEMS, RIGHTING WRONGS

In our discussion in chapter 3 on the various family styles pictured by the circumplex, we mentioned the need of each style to learn problem-solving skills. Despite the type of family structure involved, appropriate problem solving is a major missing factor in dysfunctional families.

Conflict resolution relates directly to satisfaction in marriage. The strategy that produces the least satisfaction is withdrawal: One or both of the parties involved refuse to discuss the issue or pretend it doesn't exist. Next come husbands and wives who approach conflict believing that only one person can be right, and the other one must be wrong. This attitude increases tension in a marriage; when one partner loses, the relationship loses. Next, we find couples who believe that resolving conflicts involves a form of compromise where one gives in to the wishes of the other. None of these methods lead to a high degree of marital happiness. Just how do people go about solving problems in a mature and satisfactory way?

First, *couples with good conflict resolution skills see conflict as beneficial.* Conflict need not pose a threat to the marriage, nor does it necessarily suggest that something is wrong within the relationship. God gave us two eyes that see different pictures and a brain that reconciles these pictures. In the same way, He gave partners in marriages the ability to view an issue in at least two ways. Solving problems means finding a way to reconcile the differing viewpoints.

Second, *mature couples attack the problem and not the people involved.* They realize that problems don't reside "in" people, so they are free to look for solutions instead of looking for someone to blame.

Third, *mature people give up the need to be right.* They never try to coerce others into agreement with them. Instead, they see differences of opinion as a way of looking at alternate solutions to a particular situation. They ask, "How many options are there for overcoming this obstacle?" This prevents the problem from turning into a power struggle.

Fourth, *couples with healthy conflict resolution skills allow each other to express all thoughts, opinions, feelings, and desires, and give serious consideration to the other's viewpoint.* Some Christians have difficulty sharing their desires—what they want in a particular instance—believing that personal desires and wants demonstrate a selfish nature. However, God wants to give us the desires of our hearts (Psalm 37:4). We can freely share what we want, as long as we don't demand that our partner meet our wishes.

CONFRONTING TO CORRECT
Suffering in silence, a common problem in marriage, is a form of lying. We commit a sin of omission by not sharing the truth, allowing our partner to know the small (or possibly large) hurts that we feel. A wife may fear sharing her anger or hurt feelings with her husband, or a husband may expect his wife to read his mind—or vice versa. Whatever the reason for not confronting, if you put on a sweet smile and tell your partner that nothing is wrong, you are lying. Your silence only enlarges the pain and possible misunderstanding. Partners who remain silent when hurt often fall into the trap of keeping score, adding each new offense to a mental list of grievances. No sharing takes place, no healing occurs. This is in direct contrast to 1 Corinthians 13:5, "[Love] is not rude, it is not self-seeking, it is not easily angered, *it keeps no record*

of wrongs" (emphasis added). If the offended partner waits for the other to come and apologize, a stalemate can quickly set in.

The solution to this situation lies in following the steps outlined in Matthew 18:15-17 and Matthew 5:23-24. These verses, often ignored and seldom applied to the marriage union, deal with confronting a brother who sins against you. Both passages state that the responsibility for clearing up a problem rests with both parties. If one party doesn't confront, the other must.

By combining the steps of Matthew 18:15-17 with the conflict resolution skills discussed earlier, marriage partners have a method for dealing with even the most entrenched behavior. Proper confrontation involves speaking for yourself and sharing what you feel without blaming anyone else. It leaves room for explanations that you may not have considered and for your partner's feelings in the matter. It takes seriously the warning in Galatians 6:1 — check your own spirituality first, be gentle, and watch out for temptation.

If good communication and conflict resolution don't produce satisfactory results, the confronting partner may then follow step two and bring in a second person as a witness. This witness should be someone skillful in negotiating and well-respected by both partners, someone who understands the need for clear, open communication in a marriage. If the offending partner still does not respond, then the confronting partner should follow the last, and most difficult step. He or she should bring the situation to the attention of the pastor or elders in their church. Because many churches today shrink from the biblical duty of Christian discipline, a professional counselor may need to be consulted instead.

GUIDELINES FOR CHANGE
For those who merely need to "redecorate" their marriages as a necessary first step toward becoming more effective parents, we offer some suggestions for bringing about positive changes in the marriage subsystem:

√ Recognize the uniqueness of your mate, and the value

he or she represents before God. Accept your husband or wife as a gift from God to you and ask Him to help you appreciate the other's weaknesses as well as strengths.

✓ Allow your partner to have thoughts and feelings different from yours and reserve the right to think and feel for yourself only. Learn to respond to *what* is said and not to *how* it is said.

✓ Express your wants and desires openly, sharing your thoughts and feelings, but not demanding to have your way. Give your mate the right to have dreams and desires.

✓ Study the problem-solving skills discussed earlier in this chapter and decide to practice them. It may seem awkward at first, and you may fail and have to start over, but make a start and keep on trying.

✓ Focus on changing yourself, not your spouse. Attempting to change a spouse always produces resistance. Don't try to make too many changes at once. Work on only one area at a time. Don't move on to a new area until the changes you've made begin to feel comfortable.

✓ Be willing to face your own mistakes and failures in the relationship. Yield to God the need to be right, and learn to ask for forgiveness. Talk with your mate about goals for your relationship, and make a commitment to accomplish those goals.

✓ Be clear about expectations; clarify meanings of words spoken and implied. Don't assume you understand or know what your mate is thinking—God does not give any of us the ability to read another's mind, not even someone we live intimately with for years.

✓ Expect not to be perfect, but keep on trying. Allow your partner the same freedom not to be perfect; be gentle, as Christ was gentle, in your dealings with your mate.

✓ Most importantly, *remember that we can modify our behavior, but it is God who must work the changes permanently into our lives.* Romans 8:29 tells us that God is creating the image of Christ in all His children. He often uses our mates as grindstones in this process. How is He using your mate to accomplish this change of image in your life?

Practice the scriptural principles for marriage, and expect God to bless your efforts and to reward you with a more satisfying and fulfilling relationship. But, what if you do all this, seek the help of a counselor, follow all the advice you are given, and your mate still doesn't respond? The chapter on single parenting will offer help for those in this situation.

MARRIAGE TRAINING

Proverbs 22:6 could be called the Christian parents' motto: "Train a child in the way he should go, and when he is old he will not turn from it." We often fail to realize that training a child involves what we *do* much more than what we *say*. Training a child in the way he should go includes not only giving guidance but modeling godliness in daily interaction with the family. Teach your child what a well-functioning marriage looks like and how a well-structured family works. A child must grow up *feeling* the structure; demonstrate it to him daily. Parent-child relationships, even good ones, cannot make up for what the marriage subsystem lacks. Remember, *your marriage is more important than your role as a parent.*

BUILDING ON THE FOUNDATION

Many of the same skills you develop in creating a stable marriage can help you be an effective parent. Not only will you be modeling a good relationship for your children, but you can make use of these skills in your interaction with them. As you build your family on the foundation of your marriage, you establish a strong family identity that gives a child an anchor when he or she faces demanding peer pressure.

CHAPTER SIX

REMEDIAL PARENTING 101

One mother, upon being told how lucky she was to have such fine children, responded, "Luck, my foot. It took a lot of hard work!" If parents agree on anything, they agree that parenting requires years of emotional and physical labor. When God said, "Blessed is the man whose quiver is full of [children]" (Psalm 127:5), He chose not to mention sleepless nights and teenage rebellion.

God created man and woman in His image and told them to be fruitful and multiply and fill the earth. This may be the only command He ever gave that mankind has carried out successfully. But for many parents the success stops there, for God desires that we fill the earth not just with children, but with godly offspring. Our God-given task as parents is to mold into our children's lives the character of Christ. How? By "bring[ing] them up in the nurture and admonition of the Lord" (Ephesians 6:4, KJV). In other words, by finding the balance between unconditional love and godly training, teaching, and instructing. Throughout Scripture, we find promises of help, strength, and wisdom. God, as our perfect parent, clearly defines His expectations of us, and also gives us Himself as an example to follow.

The Old Testament provides us with insight into the origin of family systems. Since God created the system, we can look to Him for an example of how it works. Exodus 20:5-6 states: "For I, the Lord your God, am a jealous God, visiting the iniquity of the fathers on the children, on the third and the fourth generations of those who hate Me, but showing loving-kindness to thousands, to those who love Me and keep My commandments" (NASB). These verses are not a prophecy, but a warning about the effects of sin on children.

God holds individuals responsible for their own sins. Nevertheless, children reap some of the punishment by virtue of their spiritual heritage — the behavior of the parents rubs off on the children. Alcoholism, physical abuse, incest, even attitudes shown toward spouses, all run through families from one generation to the next. If your father called your mother his "old lady" and treated her like dirt under a doormat, chances are you've brought that same attitude into your own marriage. Unless you make some changes now, your children will perpetuate your actions. Leviticus 26:40 shows how we can redeem ourselves before God, by confessing our own sins and the sins of our parents. In order to do this we must be honest with ourselves about the seriousness of our parents' problems. We don't rationalize or make excuses for an unhealthy parent in the name of forgiveness. An abusive parent was not "just a little moody." An alcoholic parent didn't just "drink a little bit." Instead of claiming forgiveness prematurely, which often disguises denial, we bring the sins of our parents before the Lord, confess them, and look to God to help us make the necessary changes in our nuclear families. In this way, a family system can begin to turn itself around and receive God's promised blessings on those who love Him.

GOD, THE FATHER

The circumplex helps us analyze God's parenting methods. For instance, God's family is *connected*. He created an open, honest family system by hiding nothing about His chosen people. By revealing both the good and the bad about our spiritual ancestors, Scripture allows us to feel connected to the great men and women of the Bible. Each of them experienced failure and shortcomings just as we do. God provided a way for us to stay connected in James 5:16: "Confess your sins to each other and pray for each other." God even took care to make sure that Jesus, the one sinless man of all time, would understand our weaknesses, for He "has been tempted in every way, just as we are" (Hebrews 4:15). In Genesis 4:9, Cain tried to disengage himself from his family when he replied to God's question about Abel's presence, "Am I my brother's keeper?" Throughout Scripture, God makes it plain that His children are to be connected and to care for each other.

God's family is also *structured.* His loving plan for parenting includes correcting (Proverbs 3:12; 2 Timothy 3:16), instructing (Psalm 32:8; 1 Timothy 6:3), and providing for us (Psalm 68:10; 1 Timothy 6:17). He does this by establishing clear *roles* for Himself and us—He is the sovereign King, we are His subjects (Psalm 5:2). He is our Shepherd, we are His sheep (Psalm 23:1, John 10:2-4). He is the Father, we are His children (Deuteronomy 32:6; Galatians 4:6-7). As His children, we are to submit to His sovereign authority in every area of our lives (Isaiah 61:10-11; Hebrews 12:9). He also gives us clear *rules* to follow (e.g., Exodus 20:1-17; Mark 12:28-31), and assures us of His unconditional love (Psalm 103:8-10; 1 John 3:1). As a loving Father, He chastises those He loves when they choose to disobey: "My son, do not make light of the Lord's discipline, and do not lose heart when He rebukes you, because the Lord disciplines those He loves, and He punishes everyone He accepts as a son" (Hebrews 12:5-6).

Though God's rules and consequences are structured, He is not *rigid.* Consider the example of Abraham pleading with God for the safety of even 10 righteous men who might dwell in the city of Sodom (Genesis 18:16-33). Or, look at the example of Moses who interceded for the Israelites and begged God's forgiveness for them (Numbers 14). God showed His willingness to listen to intercessory prayer, to consider other viewpoints, and to change His plans. Our Heavenly Father gives us a second chance—as many times as we need it, but we must first be willing to follow the examples of Abraham and Moses. They respectfully negotiated with God. They humbled themselves and submitted to His authority, then God was willing to put aside His "rank" and listen to their pleas.

Ephesians 6:4 warns us, "Fathers, do not irritate and provoke your children to anger—do not exasperate them to resentment—but rear them [tenderly] in the training and discipline and the counsel and admonition of the Lord" (AMP). When we structure our families according to God's example, we lessen the risk of provoking our children—or allowing them to provoke us.

EXTERNAL VS. INTERNAL
The Old Testament reveals God primarily as an external God. He influenced His children, the Israelites, with external controls by outlining specific rules for their welfare, such as the Ten Commandments. These rules spelled out what to do, what not to do, and carried with them the promise of curses for disobedience and blessings for those who obeyed. God's punishment of wayward acts was sure and consistent, as was His reinstatement of Israel when they recognized their sins and repented.

In the New Testament, God changed His relationship to believers. First, He sent Jesus as the fulfillment of the external Law (Matthew 5:17-18). Then, after Christ's death and resurrection, God sent His Holy Spirit as the internal Agent who enables us to live our lives in obedience to His desires (John 14:16-18). Thus we see that our Heavenly Father began the process of raising His children using external methods. Then, according to Romans 5:6, "At just the right time, when we were still powerless, Christ died for the ungodly," and God shifted to reliance on internal controls.

As parents, we are to follow God's example with our children. Initially, parents control children from an external position by setting limits and enforcing consequences. As the children grow, they begin to internalize the teachings of their parents and become more and more responsible for making wise decisions. This then becomes a basis for responding to the indwelling voice of the Holy Spirit when they become believers in Christ and begin to grow spiritually.

PUNISHMENT VS. DISCIPLINE

God's model for correcting His children also reflects the change from external to internal methods. In the Old Testament, chastisement meant "to correct with blows, to inflict pain." This corresponds with our definition of the word *punishment: presenting something negative or taking away something positive with the purpose of eliminating or reducing an undesirable behavior.* In other words, someone big imposing their will on someone small. As you can imagine, this loses its effectiveness when the small someone gets bigger than the big someone. With punishment, the control is external; it teaches what not to do in a situation, but it generally fails to tell what behavior to put in its place. We do not advocate abusive measures, but we recognize that young children need external controls; chapter 8 shares guidelines for using such controls.

In the New Testament, Jesus fulfilled the Law and came to dwell within us. We no longer have rules inscribed on stone tablets, for now God writes His Law on our hearts (Romans 2:15). This inner Law encourages self-control or *discipline: the development of a set of internal controls to govern our behavior* (2 Timothy 1:7). The process of discipline, by communicating what to do, leads to desirable behaviors.

Inner discipline requires that children learn the same problem-solving skills that we outlined for parents in chapter 5. As children grow, internal controls should begin to develop and parents should gradually work themselves out of a job. This means moving from a more *structured connected* style to a more *flexibly detached* one.

BELONGING TO "US"

We each need to belong to something bigger than we are—a family. This sense of belonging gives us an identity and helps to establish our character. Children particularly need a family structure to provide a secure environment for healthy emotional growth.

American families, even Christian ones, often don't have a sense of family identity. Many have lost touch with, and consequently respect for, their family heritage. Lacking a proper family, some children seek to satisfy this "belonging" need through peer groups and other activities. The prevalence of gangs in many urban communities may result partially from the erosion of family structure in our society.

Some children react to a lack of family structure by creating unhealthy social relationships. They may experience shyness and poor self-esteem and fail to develop good social skills. Many of those who grew up in a dysfunctional family system find themselves in codependent relationships as adults, lacking the ability to form healthy adult relationships. In contrast, those who belong to a well-functioning family system seldom struggle with self-esteem issues.

Along with family loyalty, traditions speak about the things a family stands for, the things they value. Traditions—those activities that you *always* do—help to solidify a child's feeling of being part of something special. In Christian families, the traditions of celebrating Christ's birth and resurrection and sharing the Lord's Supper serve as reminders of the uniqueness of our relationship to God, our Father. In the same way, continuing some traditions from your childhood, and adding new ones with special meaning for your nuclear family, can pull the system together.

Some families have monthly, weekly, even daily rituals involving dinnertime, family worship times, or family recreation. Husbands and wives sometimes establish a tradition of a weekly date to give themselves time alone without the pressure of the children. The tradition itself is secondary; the important thing is that the family shares in activities that give a sense of belonging.

MORE BUILDING BLOCKS
Well-structured families not only respect family loyalty and share traditions, they also spend time together, affirm one

another, and work to develop emotional closeness and trust.

No adequate substitute has ever been found for simply being together. It takes time to build a strong parent-child bond just as it takes time to build our relationship with God. Unfortunately, too many parents have bought into the quality vs. quantity myth. A quality relationship without an adequate quantity of time devoted to it is difficult, if not impossible, to create. Children, especially older ones, don't relate on demand.

Times of special sharing between parent and child often come while participating in some activity together—anything from washing dishes to riding bikes to shopping. If the activity allows time and space for talking, casual conversation often turns into real sharing. Watching television, playing computer games, or other activities such as these place the focus on an external object rather than on the relationship you wish to develop. In addition, activities involving friends or other family members may not leave enough "quiet time" for personal sharing to take place.

Affirmation, another important dimension of a healthy family, gives members of the family positive feedback. It tells them that they are valued persons and that others notice their contribution to the family and appreciate them. Twice, in Matthew 3:17 and 17:5, we see God praising His Son publicly: "And a voice from heaven said, 'This is my Son, whom I love; with Him I am well pleased.' "

Jesus also received affirmation and praise from God in more private ways, such as when He read the Prophet Isaiah's words: "Here is My Servant, whom I uphold, My chosen One in whom I delight" (Isaiah 42:1). God modeled affirmation for His Son and showed us how to build up a child. Our children need both public and private proof of our pleasure with them. Affirmation comes in many forms. A word of praise, a smile, a gentle hug, or a special birthday celebration can make a child feel approved and secure. Unique (and appropriate) nicknames can encourage children and remind them that they are special people.

Emotional closeness and trust come as a result of spending

time together, resolving conflicts, and receiving affirmation. Trust also depends on the consistency of parents' actions and attitudes. Consistency means following through on all verbal instructions and warnings, and keeping the rules of the system clear. Parents who discipline or punish unpredictably run the risk of frustrating their children and failing to gain their children's confidence.

Parents also must consistently show respect for their children. Children find it hard to believe in a parent's love when they are belittled, shamed, teased, or threatened with abandonment. Consider the attitude of your Heavenly Father toward you: "Never will I leave you; never will I forsake you," and, "Jesus Christ is the same yesterday and today and forever" (Hebrews 13:5, 8).

Contact with other families is another characteristic common to healthy, well-structured families. Families benefit from sharing with others in their times of fun and times of need. Children need to watch healthy adult relationships at work and see how other families function. Scripture clearly mandates interaction with others in such "one another" passages as Romans 12:4-18.

BACK TO THE DRAWING BOARD

Creating a well-functioning family calls for parents to assume their God-given parental authority and parental agreement. In chapter 4, we stated that Scripture does not show a hierarchy within the executive subsystem. In a family with children, however, a definite hierarchy should exist. This hierarchy serves to introduce children to the presence of authority and the act of submission to that authority. Parents must exercise authority over their children.

Many children grow up believing that when they turn 18 they will no longer have any authority figures over them. It is a fact of life, however, that as children grow up, an ever-increasing number of authority figures enter their lives — teachers, policemen, coaches, bosses, and on and on. Children who learn to submit to their parents have the ability to submit to other authorities as well. And when children are introduced to God, they find it much easier to submit to His sovereignty in their lives if they first have learned to submit to their parents. We will go into more detail about parental authority in chapter 7.

Effective parenting requires that parents establish rules, exercise control over their children by enforcing consequences, and join together in an agreed-on parenting plan. Parental agreement means presenting a united front, speaking with one voice when nurturing and admonishing your children. It means being "one" as God the Father, Jesus the Son, and the Holy Spirit are one (John 17:11, 21). Parental agreement does not mean that parents necessarily feel the same feelings or think the same thoughts—that would demand enmeshment. Instead, agreement indicates that parents have become mutually submissive (Ephesians 5:21) and have resolved any differences regarding parenting strategies. They then commit themselves to a unified parenting game plan.

Agreement between parents is an important aspect of consistency. Children should know the rules and the consequences of breaking them. They also should know that there is a 100 percent probability of the consequence being carried out—regardless of which parent is in the role of authority at the time.

Parental authority and agreement require a blending of the parenting styles that the husband and wife brought with them into marriage. Most new parents start doing "what comes naturally" and then discover that what comes naturally to them doesn't agree with their spouse's ideas of raising children. When this happens, it's time to take a careful look at the methods used in your families of origin. Decide which of those methods, if any, were effective and agree to abandon the ineffective ones.

In our family therapy experience, we have observed that children develop some of their most serious problems in response to parents who fail to come to agreement about parenting methods. Parental agreement is not an optional item in the parents' bag of tricks. It is a major factor in rearing emotionally healthy children. When parents don't commit themselves to solving disagreements, even small ones, they empower their children to do just as they please. Consequently, at some point in a child's development, symptoms begin to appear which may include such things as hyperactivity, disrespect for authority, and school problems. Parents should strive to settle all disagreements about the nature of a misdeed, or the type of correction required. Endless arguing about methods of discipline teaches children to play one parent against the other. Even the most angelic child can become a master at this if confronted often with parents' unresolved conflicts.

BREAKING THE PATTERNS OF THE PAST
If you have completed your genogram and circumplex tests, you should have a clear idea of the effective and ineffective patterns of parenting learned from your family of origin. Ineffective parenting methods include such things as punishing in anger and giving too many warnings (which usually leads to punishing in anger). Constantly reminding children to do something produces parents who think for their children, rather than children who think for themselves. Other futile measures involve shaming children into submissive behavior, threatening them with abandonment, and yelling. Shaming a child produces emotional withdrawal and is abusive. As you and your spouse study your families of origin, you may come up with other examples of harsh or unsuccessful parenting methods.

To break the ties with past ineffective parenting styles, you must have new methods ready to take their place. Also, you must be completely committed to carrying out the new methods consistently. In Matthew 12:43-44, Jesus tells a parable about driving an evil spirit out of a man. The spirit goes off, but can find no place to rest. "Then [the evil spirit] says, 'I will return to the house I left.' When it arrives, it finds the house unoccupied, swept clean and put in order. Then it goes and takes with it seven other spirits more wicked than itself, and they go in and live there. And the final condition of that man is worse than the first."

The failure of the man in this parable to put anything in the evil spirit's place left him open to a more severe condition than he experienced at first. It is imperative that you have a plan clearly outlined before you attempt changes in your parenting style.

DRAWING A BLUEPRINT

What is your motive for training your children? Do you want to keep them from inconveniencing you? Is your goal in parenting simply to maintain control over your children until they turn 18 and then hope that they can make it in the "real world"? Or, do you want to mold your children into adults with godly character?

Training up godly children requires a mental picture of the desired result before beginning the task of parenting. Without that picture, parenting is like trying to build a house without a blueprint. Haphazardly nailing boards together doesn't produce a well-built structure. Likewise, randomly applying tools of discipline, without a clear picture of the target objective, doesn't produce well-behaved children. Instead, it causes children to become frustrated, angry, and confused.

God once again gives us an example to follow. He knows the type of people He wants us to be and what it will take to make us resemble the end product. In Romans 8:29, God gives us a glimpse of His blueprint: "For those God foreknew He also predestined to be conformed to the likeness of His Son, that He might be the firstborn among many brothers." God plans to mold His children into the image of Jesus Christ, and all of His training and discipline serve that purpose. It is this same image of Christ that we are to hold in our minds as we work to shape our children's character.

Many people enter parenthood desiring to raise their children to be "better" people than they themselves. However, Luke 6:40 says: "A student is not above his teacher, but everyone who is fully trained will be like his teacher." If you wish your children to be better people, then you must become a better person yourself.

Spiritually lukewarm parents often produce doubt and rejection of faith in their children and hinder their spiritual development. In order to train children according to God's example, parents must have a vibrant, active relationship with Christ. As parents walk closely with Christ, they will learn what characteristics they want to build into the lives of their children. Such things as honesty, a sense of justice, mercy, and a desire to share with others come to mind quickly when one thinks of being Christlike. But there are many facets to Christ's character.

In Matthew 11:29, Jesus offers His only description of Himself: "Take My yoke upon you, and learn of Me; *for I am meek and lowly in heart:* and ye shall find rest unto your souls" (KJV, emphasis added). What does it mean to be meek and lowly of heart? Perhaps this would be a good place to begin a study of Christ's character.

Wherever you begin your study, it is vital that you start now to identify key character qualities, behaviors, and habits that you want to instill in your children. Then work to build those qualities and behaviors into your life first. "A righteous man who walks in his integrity—how blessed are his sons after him" (Proverbs 20:7, NASB).

ACCOMPLISHING YOUR PURPOSE

Children spend approximately 18 years in a type of apprenticeship with their family of origin. An apprentice is a learner who, for a specified period, serves under a master craftsman to learn a particular skill. The master gives verbal instruction, supervision, and demonstrations. This is an ongoing, continuous process as opposed to a sporadic series of events. Working side by side with the teacher, the student receives frequent feedback on the progress made. Ultimately, the apprentice is ready to function independently of his teacher.

As the master craftsmen in our children's lives, we have been instructed to "train a child in the way he should go, and when he is old he will not turn from it" (Proverbs 22:6). Deuteronomy 6:6-7 gives instructions for the apprenticeship process: "These commandments that I give you today are to be upon your hearts. Impress them on your children. Talk about them when you sit at home and when you walk along the road, when you lie down and when you get up."

This passage also gives us some idea of what our curriculum should be as we guide our children in the way they should go. As we perform the day-to-day chores of living, we are to train our children to think with biblical minds. This means imparting basic scriptural principles and sharing how these affect us. It means going beyond verbal instruction by modeling morality and righteous living, teaching our children to see God's hand at work in our own lives first.

John 1:1 tells us, "In the beginning was the Word, and the Word was with God, and the Word was God." First, God gave the Word—the rules and the understanding of what is right. Then the Word became flesh—God became Jesus to role-model rightness for us. It's not sufficient to simply structure your family according to scriptural rules and principles. You have to live them. You must "become" your own word.

Parents can go to an extreme in modeling, doing a great job of building family bonds and affirming their children, yet fail to teach Scripture. At the other extreme, rigid parents often try to cram values down a child's throat without concern for the lifestyle they model. Children need both a knowledge of the Word and a godly example to prepare them for adulthood. Trying to force children to think what you want them to think only plants the seeds of rebellion. We will deal more with the causes of rebellion in chapter 14.

PARENTING ADULT CHILDREN

As family therapists, we often hear statements like, "I will stay in this marriage till the kids are gone." Parents mistakenly assume that parenting ends when the children grow up, leave home, and begin lives and families of their own. It's true that parents no longer supervise their adult children's lives, but function more as consultants. However, the role modeling never stops. Even after children marry, parents can continue to teach their children by example how to deal with the conflicts of daily life together. It is never too late, or unnecessary, to strengthen your marriage relationship.

BUILDING FENCES

Healthy family systems require the building of some fences. Fences serve many purposes. They define spaces; they provide privacy and give protection; they can shut out people or hem them in, sometimes against their will. Fences in family systems, known as *boundaries*, work much the same way. Some are useful and maintain harmony and balance; some are divisive and create tension. What kinds of boundaries should exist in a family? And where should they be? Chapter 7 looks at the proper boundaries for a family and considers some problems that commonly occur in family systems.

CHAPTER SEVEN

PROBLEMS IN THE SYSTEM

In chapter 4 we talked about a small unit within a family, made up of the husband and wife or a single parent, called the *executive subsystem.* Many other subsystems exist in a family with children; the number of subsystems depends on the number of children and, in the case of divorce and remarriage, the number of parents. Each parent forms a subsystem with each child, as well as each child with another child.

Parent/child subsystems serve the purpose of modeling and apprenticeship, with children learning not only life skills but also obedience, submission, and respect for authority.

SUBSYSTEMS AND BOUNDARIES

Genograms allow for easy identification of subsystems. Simply draw a dotted line around each unit of two family members. When you draw a dotted line around each subsystem, you also indicate some of the *boundaries* that should rightfully exist. Boundaries are like fences—they define borders around subsystems and around each individual in the system [see figure 13]. Most fences have gates; some swing in one direction, some swing back and forth. Some gates are locked and only certain people hold the key. Occasionally, a fence will have no gate at all. Fences can be two feet high or seven feet high with barbed wire on the top.

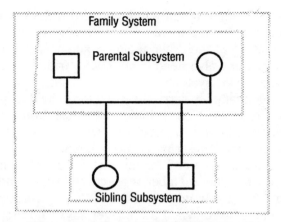

Figure 13. Typical Family Boundaries

In families, individuals and subsystems function, or mal-function, within the boundaries they establish. Individual boundaries regulate the amount of "space" allowed between people in a relationship. Boundaries exist around subsystems of two or more people and the closeness or distance between them can be measured on the cohesion scale of the circumplex. The adaptability scale of the circumplex, showing a family's reaction to change, relates to boundaries around families. Rigid families build a brick boundary around the family, immovable and unchangeable. Chaotic families tend to draw chalk lines in the grass that blow away and change daily.

Generally, a boundary has a two-directional gate that keeps issues in that need not be shared with others, but also allows others to cross over and relationships to develop. At times, however, a boundary may not be as permeable in each direction, allowing things in but not out or vice versa. Sometimes family members build boundaries so high and closed that no one is allowed inside.

Boundaries should exist between family members. In some enmeshed families, boundaries don't exist at all except around the entire family system. Members become absorbed into each other; their emotions and roles become entwined. At the same time, the impermeable boundary around the family system shuts out any influence from the outside. Individual family members need privacy; they need to think their own thoughts, feel their own feelings, and perform their God-given roles. They also need contact with friends and families beyond their own system.

Disengaged families carry the need for individual privacy to the other extreme. They build individual boundaries like stone walls and shut each other out, while no boundary exists around the family system. Healthy boundaries are porous; they allow for privacy and for interaction, but they are never violated. Each family member respects the rights and feelings of the others: Each honors the others as worthwhile and valuable individuals. When a teenager says "no" to drugs or sex, he is establishing a boundary around himself. When parents say "no" to a child's misbehavior, they are establishing boundaries within the family.

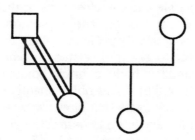

Figure 14. Genogram Showing an Incestuous Relationship

Families violate boundaries in a number of ways. Sometimes one family member violates the boundaries of another, as in physical abuse or incest [see figure 14; the triple line indicates an overinvolved relationship]. At other times, in chaotic or enmeshed families, boundaries don't exist where they are needed. In these situations, parents may demand information or action from a child that violates a personal boundary. A mother may insist that her child tell her every-thing, yet the mother doesn't tell the child anything at all — even information the child is entitled to hear. Children violate the executive subsystem boundary by getting caught in the middle of parental conflicts [see figure 15; the double line represents a close relationship]. Sometimes parents allow the children to have an equal vote with their marriage partner, a situation which occurs commonly in recast families, but is not exclusive to them. Children can only permeate the executive subsystem when the parents are ineffectual in establishing a marriage boundary or the boundary simply is not well-defined. Allowing children to violate the marriage boundary can cause disintegration within the marriage.

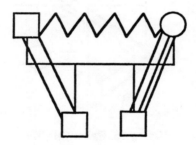

Figure 15. Triangulation of Child in Marital Conflict

CREATING TRIANGLES

When friction occurs in any subsystem, a unique process takes place — *triangulation*. Triangulation happens when a conflict exists between two people and a third person is drawn in to relieve the tension. In triangulation, two people act in *collusion* — planning and acting together in secrecy — against a third person, even though none of them may be aware of what they are doing or why. Collusions can be very subtle, but are particularly dysfunctional when a child is forced to take sides against one of his own parents. Because of the need for a strong marital unit, collusions between a parent and child against another parent devastate not only the system, but the individual participants as well [see figure 16; the dashes represent a distant relationship, while the jagged line represents a conflictual one]. In these triangles, the parents manage to keep the focus off the missing elements in their own relationship. Instead of involving the children in the marriage subsystem, parents need to focus on resolving conflict, and developing problem-solving and communication techniques that will enhance the marriage.

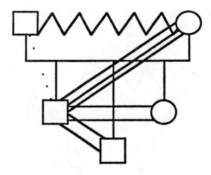

Figure 16. Parental Child

Triangulation is a learned behavior, a habit formed in one's family of origin. When anxiety occurs, we naturally seek to escape the tension. One way of doing this is to create a triangle by drawing someone else into the problem. The way you dealt with conflict in your family of origin influences the way you will deal with conflict in your nuclear family. The work you did on your genogram and circumplex should reveal any patterns of triangulation and the methods of conflict resolution learned in your childhood. Most of us as children learn to play one of three roles: victim, rescuer, or persecutor. We then carry this role into our adulthood and continue to play the same role in our nuclear families.

Triangles work in a variety of ways. Parents in a tense

marriage may concentrate on their common problems with a misbehaving child, or use a child as a sounding board for their complaints about each other. When Mom complains to her daughter about her husband, instead of confronting him directly, she has pulled her child into a triangle. Sometimes parents who are frustrated and angry with each other will release these emotions on their children, using them as a scapegoat, instead of resolving their own conflict. Some children experience such anxiety when parents fight that they step in to "help" the parents end the argument and restore peace to the family.

In a slightly different scenario, when a mother and child have an argument, Dad gets angry with either the child or his wife and steps in. The focus of the conflict is now deflected and the mother and child do not resolve their conflict with each other. Instead, the child feels picked on by both parents and the mother feels undermined by her husband. The original conflict still exists but has now been complicated.

At times, a child, sensing tension between his parents, may develop behavioral problems in order to draw attention away from the marriage relationship [see figure 15]. Physical symptoms may also develop in children. A child who suffers from asthma may experience an attack in an unconscious attempt to distract his quarreling parents from their conflict. The tension in the marriage didn't cause the asthma, but triggered the attack. This is an effort on the part of the child to relieve the fear and insecurity of having parents who won't resolve their conflicts in a mature manner.

Some couples who fail to establish a relational boundary around their marriage which will separate them from their families of origin may draw their parents into a triangle and complicate their marriage issues. Parents who fail to establish intimacy and a boundary around the marriage bed end up with children who are in the middle of the marriage. The parents never have time alone together. The failure to establish a boundary around the marital bed may actually encourage incest. Very severe symptoms can result from failure to establish appropriate boundaries.

Grandparents sometimes get triangulated into a nuclear family, siding with the grandchildren against their parents [see figures 17]. Another common triangle occurs when a parent steps in between two warring siblings, takes sides, and judges without all the facts. Parents can use times of argument between children beneficially by teaching conflict resolution skills without taking sides against either child.

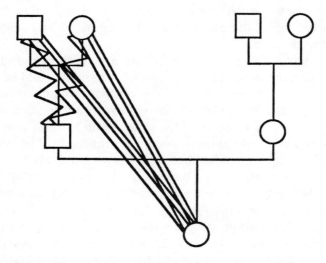

Figure 17. Grandparents Crossing Generational Boundaries

In chapter 2, we presented the genogram of Joseph's family (see pages 27-31). The six-generation genogram provides multiple examples of triangulation. Perhaps the most obvious one includes Joseph, his father Jacob, and all of Joseph's brothers (as a unit). One can easily see the destructiveness of triangles by studying the relationships in that Old Testament family.

Whatever type of triangle is involved, the outcome is the same: The original pair fail to resolve the conflict between them. The healing and understanding which needs to take place between them never occurs.

BREAKING OUT

Triangles don't work. They interfere with healthy conflict resolution, and prevent real understanding between family members. When a third family member gets involved in a relationship between two others, they merely succeed in getting caught in the crossfire.

To avoid forming triangles, family members must deal with conflict directly, speaking the truth in love and forgiving one another (Ephesians 4:15, 25, 32). How do you get out of triangles and collusions once they are already formed? Remember that major relationships should not cross generational lines. If you are closer to a son or daughter than to your spouse, a triangle probably exists. Next, listen to your conversations with others. Do you spend much of your time talking about another family member? Do you find yourself taking sides with someone against another person? You are caught in a triangle. You need to examine your relationships within your family and look for unresolved conflict.

When a triangle exists, it is a sure sign that a conflict resides with at least two of the three people involved. Identify those who are in conflict. Then the third party must withdraw or be removed, and the two people in conflict must accept the responsibility for resolving the problems in their own relationship. The conflict must be dealt with directly as commanded in Matthew 18:15-17. When, in the course of following the prescribed steps in Matthew 18, a third party is required, this person is brought in openly, not in a secret collusion. The three parties then sit down together and work to resolve the conflict. Professional family therapists may be able to help in this process; family members can seldom help without getting trapped in a triangulated position.

POWER VS. AUTHORITY

Chapter 6 dealt briefly with parental authority. Because authority is equated with power, we find that much confusion exists concerning the use of authority. These two terms are not identical. *Power* is the ability to impose your will on another individual by influencing him or her to do something they ordinarily would not have done. Power is limited by your physical ability to follow through. A gun may increase your physical ability, but a bullet-proof vest on the other person limits your influence on that person.

Authority is the ability to bring all the power necessary to bear on a situation to create change or influence another person's behavior. Authority incorporates the use of power beyond your own personal resources, and is limited only by the extent of your commitment.

Picture yourself driving a big rig down the freeway in your home state. The posted speed limit is 65, but you're running a little late and traffic is light, so you boost your speed to 80. You crest a hill and pick up more speed as you begin the descent. Off in the distance, you see a vehicle sitting by the side of the road. When you get a little closer you recognize the familiar black and white car of the Highway Patrol.

You begin to brake, slowing your speeding truck and gearing down. As you draw nearer, you see the patrolman step from his car, place his hat on his head, and straighten his belt. He steps to the rear of his patrol car and raises his hand to signal you to pull over. What do you do? You pull over, roll down the window, and address the officer as "sir." Why? It wasn't power that stopped you. If the officer had stepped in front of your truck he would have become another stripe on the road. On the contrary, the recognition of the authority behind the officer's badge stopped your truck.

What would have happened if you had refused to stop? The issue of power would then have come into play. The officer's commitment to bring all the power necessary to bear on the situation would have prompted him to call for some heavy-duty reinforcements. The strength of his commitment will get the truck stopped one way or another. From the moment that officer stepped out of his patrol car, he did what we call claiming the victory in advance. After that, it was just a matter of working out the details!

When you declare to your children that they will go to bed at 9:00, they will take a bath, they will get off the telephone, have you made a commitment to use all the power necessary? Have you claimed the victory from the start? Are you willing to go the distance to bring their behavior to a point of change? Once you've established that, the next step is to teach your children that there are only two ways of doing things: the easy way and the hard way. The outcome is going to be the same. That's exercising authority.

AUTHORITY AND RESPECT

Throughout a person's life, occasions arise that call for submission to authority. One never outgrows the need for obedience in certain areas of life. Christians especially must demonstrate submission to God and His commandments for His children. Hebrews 5:7-8 tells us that Jesus' prayers to His Father were heard because He was submissive, and that "although He was a son, He learned obedience from what He suffered." We cannot expect to learn obedience to our Father any other way, nor can we expect our children to learn to obey by any other method. This doesn't mean that we must be harsh in our punishment, only that we must follow through with our plan. Sometimes that will mean going against our children's wishes in order to accomplish what we know will be better for them in the end.

Parents face a demanding task: modeling for children the godly lifestyle of a follower of Christ; teaching them to think with biblical minds; consistently applying the nurture and admonition needed to keep their behavior under control. But, when parents follow the scriptural guidelines while depending on the strength and help of the Holy Spirit, then they make it easier for their children to respect them. If we do not become weary then "at the proper time we will reap a harvest if we do not give up" (Galatians 6:9). And the harvest reaped is not only respectful children, but also well-behaved children who understand the structure and importance of the family unit.

ACTION VS. REACTION

Many parents make the mistake of waiting for their children to misbehave before taking control. They then react to the behavior of their child. We see examples of this in our offices every day. Samantha's parents came in for a consultation when Samantha was about 18 months old. Like all children that age, she had an incredibly curious mind and an extremely short attention span. As we visited with her parents, Samantha proceeded to toddle around the office, inspecting various objects and pulling books off the shelves. During our consultation time, first one parent and then the other admonished Samantha to stop touching or stop pulling or stop making a mess, and to come sit down. Very little was accomplished between us and the parents or between the parents and Samantha. Unfortunately, Samantha's parents left feeling that their time had been wasted.

The parents of Calvin, a 22-month-old toddler, presented a refreshingly different scene. Mom arrived with a bag of toys and non-messy snacks to occupy Calvin's time. As we chatted with the parents, Mom would reach into her bag and pull out a toy or snack for Calvin. Before Calvin had exhausted his attention span with the object at hand, Mom would extract another goody from her bag and hand it to Calvin. She retrieved the last object, and replaced it in her bag for later use. Calvin played happily this way for our entire session.

The actions of Calvin's and Samantha's parents demonstrate active and reactive parenting. Active parenting tells the child what to do; it defines the rules and consequences so that a child knows what is expected of him. Reactive parenting merely tells the child what not to do. Samantha's parents were constantly reacting to her predictable behavior. Calvin's parents, however, demonstrated that they indeed understood the mindset of toddlers and actively prepared themselves to deal with it in advance. It took preparation and attention on the part of Calvin's mom, but the planning she put into her actions left her free to concentrate on our session and kept her youngster entertained and happy at the same time.

COMMON MISTAKES IN PARENTING
A number of common parenting mistakes thrive in today's families. Frequently, one parent assumes more than his or

her normal responsibility and overfunctions as a parent and as a spouse. The other parent then begins to slack off, delegates more responsibility to the spouse, and becomes an underfunctioner.

Family systems always strive to maintain balance. The more one partner overfunctions, the more the other will underfunction. Unfortunately, in American families, fathers usually become the family underfunctioner. As a result, everyone loses. The children end up with role models of dysfunctional parenting styles. Mom resents having to do all the emotional, and possibly physical, work of the family. Dad resents Mom for usurping his role—even though he gave it up without a fight. This unspoken conspiracy to accept dysfunctional roles is an example of a codependent relationship.

Prevention lies in refusing to overfunction in the first place. If underfunctioning partners fail in their responsibility, the burden rests on their shoulders, and they must suffer the consequences of their action—or lack of it, as the case may be. The partner who tends to overfunction may find it difficult to take this stance, and may need some coaching from a family therapist to carry it out.

Another common mistake occurs when a child is singled out to shoulder the responsibility of a parent. These *parental children* must assume an undue amount of an absent or underfunctioning parent's obligation to the family. Parental children frequently grow up to be overfunctioners in their nuclear families, and perpetuate the cycle into the next generation. They have been trained and rewarded for a particular role identity in their family of origin and taught what to expect of a spouse. The training and expectations create the perfect combination of conditions to perpetuate the cycle.

Underfunctioning often occurs when a parent fails to understand the "dailyness" of disciplining and nurturing children. Many things can interfere with daily discipline. Low self-esteem may prevent a parent from taking the role of authority and maintaining control. Some parents labor under the mistaken belief that children should just "behave" without being told what to do or having to be corrected. These parents may have been very compliant children themselves, requiring little correction or repetition of instructions. Sometimes, parents may just be too tired to be consistently alert for discipline and nurturing opportunities.

Lack of parental agreement, over- and underfunctioning, and the breakdown of parental boundaries often result in erosion of parental authority in the eyes of the children. Two other misunderstandings can lead to the undermining of authority as well. Both of these deal with the "fairness" myth. Children frequently complain, "That's not fair." Parents who try to live up to their children's idea of fairness find themselves lost in an impossible maze. The truth is, Scripture does not contain a "fairness" doctrine. Matthew 5:45 says, "He causes His sun to rise on the evil and the good, and sends rain on the righteous and the unrighteous." Life happens, and much of it seems unjustified. We do our children no favor by hiding this fact from them. While we must be careful not to show preference to one child over another, we can ignore most of their cries of unfairness.

Closely related to the notion of fairness is the issue of children and their right to "own" property. Very few states consider minors as owning property; in fact, some states still consider children as property! Regardless of how the child acquired the property in question, the child does not own it. As long as a child is under the authority of the parents, whatever the child possesses is at the grace of the parents. Cries of "It's my property," or, "Stay out of my room," are attempts by the child to undermine the authority of one or both parents. While we don't advise going too far with this, parents do have the right to take things away from a child for the purpose of admonishment.

CLEANING UP THE LEFTOVERS

Perhaps the most common mistake of all is the failure to deal with emotions, allowing leftovers to collect and fester in the minds of both parents and children. Leftovers become a problem when parents fail to recognize the need to apologize to their children when mistakes are made. Matthew 5:24-25 urges us to reconcile differences quickly. Lack of conflict resolution makes the leftovers even messier. When offenses are not dealt with quickly and reconciliation does not follow discipline, parents and children both can fall into a pattern of harboring resentments. Children need to talk about their feelings, especially when they believe they have been misunderstood or mistreated. After a time of correction, children benefit from discussions with their parents about the misdeed and the discipline administered. This can relieve much of the frustration children experience if they are unclear about why they were punished. Children need their parents' reassurance of constant love and forgiveness for any misdeed. Children also need to be taught to come to parents and ask forgiveness for disobedience, rather than pouting and waiting for parents to make amends.

Parents should take care to communicate that they don't dislike their children—just what they did. Separating the deed from the doer is a difficult, but necessary process. Carry out discipline and punishment without condemnation, without labeling the child as "bad." Parents who allow misdeeds to mount up before dealing with them run the risk of permanently identifying the child with his actions. A child ceases to tell a lie, and becomes a liar.

Punishment often becomes a time for parents to vent all their leftover resentment and frustration. Parents can avoid labeling a child with his misdeed or venting pent-up frustration by dealing quickly with each offense. Use each occasion of misbehavior as a teaching tool in the apprenticeship process by communicating scriptural truth about the nature of the offense. Talk it out, always reassuring your child of your continued love and acceptance.

FILLING UP THE PARENTAL TOOLBOX
It's time to begin applying what you have learned about the family system to the actual day-to-day chore of parenting your children. Chapter 8 lays out the foundation for setting the rules within the system and gives guidelines for using various discipline "tools."

CHAPTER EIGHT

PUTTING IT ALL TOGETHER

The lecture began as mother and son walked out of the shoe store. "Billy, I want you to take care of these shoes. I can't keep buying new ones." Billy had heard it all many times before. He let the words float undisturbed through his brain.

His mother continued. "Don't drag your feet when you're riding your bike, and for goodness sake, stay out of the mud puddles!" Something in this last statement jarred the boy to attention. He furrowed his brow, deep in thought.

"But, what if it rains?" he asked. The difficulty of it all perplexed him. Suddenly, he stopped. A flash of insight ignited his mind. Looking up at his mother, he cried, "I don't have to walk through the puddles!"

It was all perfectly clear to him now: he could walk *around* the puddles, instead of through them. Another of life's mysteries had been solved. Billy's mother also had a new insight that day: Children learn through repetition. "Order on order, order on order, line on line, line on line, a little here, a little there" (Isaiah 28:10, NASB). God has known that all along. It's the way He teaches us.

STAGES OF LEARNING
When Billy runs through life's mud puddles, to borrow Dr. James Dobson's terms, is he being willfully disobedient or

merely childishly irresponsible? The answer to that question determines the course of action when Billy arrives home with muddy shoes. At what age can parents expect their children to begin thinking for themselves? How old does a child have to be to remember the family rules from day to day—or even from hour to hour? In order to answer these questions, parents need some knowledge of child development, the stages of growth and understanding that every child of normal intellect goes through. Most parents know about "terrible twos" and "abrasive adolescence," but a parent who understands what happens in between these two stages stands a better chance of maintaining sanity.

During the first few weeks of life, a baby's needs lie in the physical realm—food, warmth, dryness—but psychological needs set in quickly. Babies need touching, rocking, and sensory stimulation. They rapidly learn to respond to their parents' emotions. During the infancy stage, the parents' main task is to impart an attitude of trust and safety to their baby. They must help the baby learn that the world, for the moment anyway, is a safe place to be and that the parents can be trusted to meet all the baby's needs.

As children approach the toddler stage, they want to do things for themselves. This desire for independence often brings with it temper tantrums and stubbornness. The parents' duty becomes one of allowing the child to experiment with his world within safe limits. Setting the limits, however, often brings a conflict between what the child "wants" and what he "needs." Parental authority first comes into play in situations where a child wants to do something beyond either his capability or the bounds of safety.

During the second year of life, children become capable of obeying simple commands and restrictions, but their memories remain short. Toddlers love to tease parents and often return to a forbidden object many times to "test" a rule. Because of this, a "no-no" must always be a "no-no" and the command must be stated clearly and patiently as often as is needed. Parents can offer the easily distractible youngster something new and safe to investigate instead.

The question "Why?" is another favorite trick of toddlers. They quickly learn that they can stall a parent's actions by asking "Why?" over and over. Toddlers cannot understand the morality behind most explanations, but do understand the firmness and consistency of a few simple rules. Children of any age need to trust their parents to control the child's behavior when the child himself cannot.

Preschool children are beginning to grasp more of an awareness of the world around them. They have a limited understanding of the differing names of things, but still lack a comprehension of time and the emotional meaning of words. Language, to them, is very concrete. When one feature of something changes, then the entire object has changed for them. For instance, a child may not recognize his Sunday School teacher away from church.

Parents of preschoolers must keep rules and consequences simple and, once again, very clear and consistent. Remember all children normally misbehave to some degree. Discipline is a daily routine in a normal healthy family, not something you do in response to failure of a child or parent to be perfect.

When children enter school, they begin the long pulling-away process that will lead them eventually to adulthood. School-age children look to their peers and others away from the family for signs of adequacy and acceptance. Parents must let go of their control over the child's environment for larger periods of time and allow the child to find his own identity apart from them. At the same time, home and family must remain a safe, comfortable place, where a child can find acceptance and love away from the stress of school and peers.

As they progress through the years of elementary school, children become more adept at handling a series of commands. A preschooler may need to be given separate, consecutive commands: come inside, wash your hands, sit down at the table. The notion of time develops slowly also. A child who dawdles at a task may just be displaying childish irresponsibility rather than disobedience. In a few years, the child will be able to remember things in a sequence. He can then be given all three instructions at once, and be expected to remember them and carry them out.

Although school-age children learn to use language to express ideas and concepts, they redefine these concepts with their own concrete interpretations and still have difficulty understanding abstract meanings. Children at this age learn to justify their actions and rationalize away misdeeds by using their own literal meaning of words: "We aren't arguing, we're discussing." Parents of school-age children must spell out very carefully the exact types of behavior that will and will not be tolerated. For instance, what actions constitute arguing? The parents must decide and tell their children clearly and concisely what is meant by "arguing" in their family. Active parenting requires that they then give the children examples of acceptable forms of expression.

The teen years continue the separation of children from their parents. Parents of teenagers should not resist their growing up but encourage them to do so, while allowing a great deal of ambivalence between childhood and adult maturity. Dealing with teenagers will be covered in chapter 14.

Regardless of the age of the child, rules must be clear and consistent, and consequences must be carried out as stated. Rules are like walls—they set limits to a space. If a child walks down a dark hallway with walls that are too close, he will try to push against them. If the walls are too far apart he will be fearful and insecure. The walls need to give a zone of comfort, not too close and not too far apart. The distance needed between walls changes as the child grows, but at all times the walls must be solid. Children must know where the limits are and know that they are firm. Limits gradually expand as children grow in ability to handle responsibility. Some of this ability comes naturally as children grow physically, but much of it comes as a result of being held accountable for their actions and being given increasingly larger responsibilities as they prove themselves capable.

WRITING THE RULES

If you've done your homework from chapter 6, you should have a clear blueprint in mind for each of your children. You should know the characteristics that you want your children to possess when they are grown. Next comes the task of writing down the rules for the family. Ideally, this should be done by both parents together, without the children present. If you have no partner, or your partner refuses to participate, chapter 9 on single-parenting offers helpful guidance.

It is imperative that you make the rules very measurable. Anyone who reads your list of rules—whether a baby-sitter, a grandparent, or your spouse—should be able to tell if your children are complying with them.

Maggie and John had two children, a boy just starting junior high and a daughter a couple of years younger. Neither parent had been consistent in disciplining the children and consequently they were beginning to reap the rewards of their lack of control.

When they sought our help in establishing some law and order in their home, we suggested they make a list of clearly stated rules and consequences. Mom and Dad really got into this project, and the next time we saw them they presented us with a detailed list. They wrote out the rules for the children concerning bedtimes, household chores, and homework. Then they spent time together as parents talking about how the rules were to be carried out. They wanted their children to respond the first time they were told to do something, and to do so without "grumbling." What did grumbling consist of? John listed the actions he considered to be grumbling: complaining, loud sighing, rolling one's eyes to the top of the head, or muttering under one's breath. For good measure, Maggie threw in using a cynical tone of voice when speaking to a parent. In addition, the parents spelled out the specific consequence for any infraction of the "no grumbling" rule—moving the wood pile from one side of the back yard to the other. John said he intended to make sure there was a full rick of wood available for the purpose all year long! It took only one evening of moving wood to make believers of both children.

Once you and your partner agree on the rules and the specific behaviors required by those rules, then the rules and consequences should be shared with the entire family as a group. Figure 18 gives some examples of rules and consequences for children at two different stages of development. Use a chart similar to this to write out your own lists. The consequences don't have to relate specifically to the misdeed, but they should be somewhat unpleasant. Consequences don't have to be "fair," that is, identical for each child. In determining consequences, take into consideration the child's temperament, age, level of responsibility, likes and dislikes. It may help, if your children are old enough to understand, to explain that you are beginning a new course of action because you have recognized that God requires you as parents to train your children to be respectful and obedient.

MAKING IT WORK

The basic principle of discipline is to use the lowest level of discomfort to get the job done. In disciplining children, as well as adults, consistency is far more important than the severity of the punishment. Consider an example: You are driving down the highway and you see a speed limit sign—*65 mph, No Tolerance.* The penalty for speeding is a $500 fine, and the temporary suspension of your driver's license. Your insurance company tends to frown on speeding tickets too, and will raise your premium. But, other cars are speeding and you're tucked in between two trucks with their radar detectors on. Even though the penalties for speeding are severe, there is little probability of getting stopped. So you set your cruise control at 71 or 72, and take your chances.

Now consider an alternative example. You are on the same highway, same warning, same penalties. But this time your car is equipped with a device set to administer a mild, but unpleasant electrical shock to the bottom of your feet and your fingertips every time your speed increases above 65 miles per hour. What do you set your cruise control on now? Probably 62 or 63, praying that you don't pick up speed as you coast downhill. Your behavior has come under control. Why? Is it the severity of the punishment or the predictability of the consequence that causes you to reduce your speed?

RULES AND CONSEQUENCES

John, age 16	
1. Clean room once a week: dust, vacuum, hang clothes, change sheets	1. Vacuum and dust entire house to Mom's specs
2. Obey curfew: 10:00 Sunday through Friday; weekend curfew will depend on type of activity	2. Loss of 10 minutes for every 1 minute late; more than 3 occurences, or 30 minutes late: loss of car keys for 3 days
3. Two hours each night of homework and review of classroom work	3. Copy word-for-word a chapter being studied
4. Attend at least 1 church youth activity a month	4. Sit with parents during church for 4 Sundays
5. Participate in at least 2 family activities a month	5. Plan and organize a family activity
6. No backtalk, sassing, or angry body language when corrected or asked to do something	6. One hour of manual labor, to be decided on by parents
Susie, age 10	
1. Make bed before school	1. Do an extra chore after school (Mom's choice)
2. Be dressed and ready for school by 7:30	2. Loss of 5 minutes play or TV time for every 1 minute late
3. Practice piano 30 minutes daily	3. Do an extra practice on Saturday
4. 30 minutes of homework and review nightly	4. Write a report on a subject you are studying
5. Feed cat daily without reminder	5. Fix own breakfast next day
6. No grumbling or complaining when asked to do something	6. Time-out, starting with 10 minutes

Figure 18. Chart of Sample Rules and Consequences for Two Ages

A highly predictable consequence, even if it is mild, is a much better deterrent to disobedience than a severe but seldom enforced punishment. Therefore, the formula to follow in choosing a discipline method is: *Choose the least severe consequence that is effective in getting the job done.*

If the consequence doesn't produce the desired result the first time, step up the penalty a little. If your child breaks his curfew, you may choose to give him a warning and cut his curfew by taking 10 minutes for every one minute late. If that isn't effective, keep increasing the time you shorten the curfew until you reach the "ouch" threshold. You must make your child uncomfortable for any discipline method to work. Hebrews 12:11 tells us, "No discipline seems pleasant at the time, but painful. Later on, however, it produces a harvest of righteousness and peace for those who have been trained by it."

One of the most frequent pleas any parent will hear, especially when there are teenagers in the house, is, "But everybody else's parents let them (fill in the blank)." When this occurs, remember two things. First, you are not responsible for everyone else's children, just your own. You must abide by your understanding of God's standards. Romans 12:2 is very clear about this: "Do not conform any longer to the pattern of this world, but be transformed by the renewing of your mind." Second, parents are still surprisingly conservative when it comes to setting rules for their children. Chances are your child's friends are trying the same plea with their own parents.

TOOLS FOR THE TOOLBOX

One of our colleagues is fond of saying, "If the only tool you have is a hammer, everything starts to look like a nail." Most parenting books give you only one "tool" to use for disciplining children. Some advocate spanking; others, negotiation or communication skills or a host of other techniques. Some of these are effective tools, others teach dangerous misinformation about parenting. Even the best tools are not effective in every situation. That's why parents need a "toolbox" full of different tools, or methods, to use in different situations. Before we begin a discussion of various effective discipline methods, let's look at some of the harmful notions that have been fostered over the years.

Many parents have read, or heard, about the problems of stifling a child's expression of his emotions. For instance, they believe that if they inhibit their child's expression of anger, they will cause some psychic trauma. This is wrong on two counts. First, unrestricted expression of anger leads to disrespect of parental, and subsequently, all authority. Scripture is clear that parents should control their children and teach them to respect authority. This is so important that Titus 1:6 warns that those who would choose to be elders or leaders in their churches must demonstrate that their children are under control.

Second, it has been proven over a period of time that the free, uninhibited expression of anger not only does not release the emotion, it actually increases the hostility level of the angry person. This is true for both parent and child. Living with an angry person affects everyone. Proverbs 22:24-25 tells us, "Do not associate with a man given to anger; or go with a hot-tempered man, lest you learn his ways, and find a snare for yourself" (NASB).

Children stand a much greater chance of psychic trauma if they are not taught to control their emotions and to express them in a healthy, non-blaming way. God recognizes the existence of angry emotions in Ephesians 4:26 but warns: "In your anger do not sin." Instead of saying, "I hate you" to a parent, a child can be taught to respond, "I'm feeling angry." That's acknowledging an honest emotion without blaming the parent for the anger.

A number of parenting methods turn the family into a democracy with children having an equal vote and sharing equal power with their parents. This is based on the humanistic notion that all people are inherently good and will turn out fine if left alone. These methods teach that parents don't have a right to impose their will on their children. However, Scripture states, "Folly is bound up in the heart of a child, but the rod of discipline will drive it far from him" (Proverbs 22:15).

Psalm 1:1 gives a rule of thumb for measuring the "rightness" of any parenting book you may read, or any method you may hear taught: "Blessed is the man who does not *walk in the counsel* of the wicked or stand in the way of sinners or sit in the seat of mockers" (emphasis added). Parents should be cautious about using a method not based solidly on Scripture and on Christian values. This doesn't mean that you have to throw the baby out with the bath water. Just run everything through the grid of Scripture, and throw out what doesn't match up. Then the truth will stand out for you to use — for all truth is God's truth, no matter who thinks he has "discovered" it.

Now, let's take a look at some effective methods for disciplining children. We'll start with the "least aversive" on our list and work our way up, as we discuss the strengths and weaknesses inherent in each method.

TALKING IT OUT

Good communication skills are an absolutely necessary addition to a parent's toolbox. Parents should know how to communicate clearly using self-responsible, non-blaming statements, without lecturing. Matthew 5:37 and James 5:12 both state that you should "simply let your 'Yes' be 'Yes,' and your 'No,' 'No.' " James 1:19 tells us to take note of this: "Everyone should be quick to listen, slow to speak and slow to become angry."

It is imperative that parents tell their children what they want, and what their plan of action will be if the children don't follow through with their end of the deal. This eliminates control talk and does away with the need for defensiveness on the part of the child.

Many times children, as well as adults, have a need to have their emotions verbally acknowledged. Children simply want to know that their parents understand what they are feeling. Once this occurs, some negative behaviors subside. Parents shouldn't try to talk their children out of a negative feeling, for there is no such thing as a "bad" emotion. Emotions are gifts from God and the feelings they produce need to be validated as real and important.

Communication skills can be misused. In humanistic models of child-raising, no limits are placed on the quality or content of the child's speech. Children can be as profane and as disrespectful as they want—in fact, it is encouraged because those words are used to get to the "deeper level of feeling."

However, parents, especially Christian ones, have a higher order of responsibility. They are to maintain a healthy family structure and establish their role of authority in their household. Allowing a child to show disrespect for either parent works against this type of structure. When a child speaks or acts disrespectfully, parents have a responsibility to say to that child, "It sounds like you're angry (or sad, upset, hurting, etc.), but I'm not accepting the way you've said that to me. That's inappropriate, that's not respectful to me." Follow the *way* the child made his remark with an appropriate consequence. After carrying out the consequence, discuss the behavior with your child and give him some examples of ways to express his emotions properly. Chapter 13 deals more specifically with communication techniques.

PRAISE AND IGNORE
This technique is more effective with younger children. Instead of zeroing in on the negative things children do and giving them negative attention, you wait until they do something positive and offer praise. If a child is coloring and sometimes scribbles and sometimes draws straight lines (and you want to reinforce the idea of drawing straight lines), rather than say,"Don't scribble," you say, "That's a nice line that you drew." This selectively reinforces and shapes the child's behavior by ignoring the negative and strengthening the positive behavior.

In Judges 6–8, we find the story of Gideon who described himself thusly: "My clan is the weakest in Manasseh, and I am the least in my family" (6:15). Yet God sent His angel to speak to Gideon and said, "The Lord is with you, *mighty warrior*" (6:12, emphasis added). God ignored Gideon's weakness and praised him for his might as a warrior. This began the process of instilling in Gideon the confidence to be used by God to defeat the Midianites.

There are some inherent disadvantages in this type of nurturing. Children sometimes need correction when they are doing negative things. It's hard to ignore deliberately spilling paint on the floor or coloring on the walls. Used wisely, however, Praise and Ignore can help a child experience success and develop positive self-esteem.

NATURAL AND LOGICAL CONSEQUENCES

These methods are included in many secular parent training programs. It allows children to make their own decisions and to experience the consequences of making bad choices. If a child does not want to wear a coat outside on a cold, winter day, the natural consequence will probably be a cold, time spent in bed, taking medicine, and perhaps missing some favorite activity. If parents don't mind having a sick child, that may be punishment enough.

Luke 15:11-32 tells the Parable of the Prodigal Son. The father of this boy allowed him to suffer the natural consequences of his choice to take his inheritance and leave home. The consequences of this decision included poverty and living with pigs. The father waited patiently for his son to come to his senses and come home, which the young man eventually did. Another example of a natural consequence is found in the Parable of the Sower in Matthew 13:1-8—the harvest is a natural consequence of planting.

Used correctly, this method can facilitate the development of decision-making, shifting the responsibility of problem solving to the child. This allows children to learn by their own experiences. When no "natural" consequences exist, parents can devise "logical" ones. These can be either rewards for fulfilling a responsibility or a punishment for not fulfilling it. For example, if a child throws clean clothes in the hamper, the child will be required to wash all the clothes.

Coming in after curfew means loss of time on the next date. Logical consequences are more directly linked to the child's behavior—they "fit" the circumstances. Because of this, the parent is better able to respond to a child's misbehavior in an impersonal way, rather than punishing out of anger. Devising logical consequences also allows the parents to use their creativity in thinking of new ways to make their children's lives uncomfortable—when circumstances call for it.

TIME OUT

Time Out is a procedure that incorporates a sequence of specific techniques designed to bring children's behavior under their own control. Children are removed from the environment where the misbehavior occurred and are placed in a *controlled environment*—in other words, a boring place— where they can contemplate their misbehavior.

The story of Jonah represents the ultimate in Time Out places. Jonah may not have been bored in the belly of the whale, but he certainly was removed from his environment! (see Jonah 1:17–2:10) Moses was also given a Time Out when God sent him to the Midian desert for 40 years (Exodus 2:15). Second Thessalonians 3:14-15 gives us a direct command: "If anyone does not obey our instruction in this letter, take special note of him. Do not associate with him, in order that he may feel ashamed. Yet do not regard him as an enemy, but warn him as a brother."

There are three important steps to the Time Out procedure:

Step #1:
Remove the child from the environment in which the unacceptable behavior has just occurred.
  √ This is a form of punishment—imposing your will on the child by eliminating the opportunity for positive reinforcement.
  √ Remove the child in a calm, objective, matter-of-fact way; avoid verbal overkill.
Step #2:
Set a specified time period for the child to remain unat-

tended and silent in Time Out.
- ✓ Keep the time period brief and age-appropriate.
- ✓ Enforce by starting the time interval over if the rules of Time Out are violated.
- ✓ If physical restraint is necessary, use the minimal force necessary and start the time interval only when the child is ready to accept responsibility for compliance with the rules.
- ✓ The *only* discussion necessary from the parent is a brief statement informing the child that the Time Out is a consequence of his/her specified behavior, and instructing the child as to the rules and expectations during the Time Out period.
- ✓ *Do not* negotiate, reason, argue, or otherwise respond to the child's statements other than to restate the previous step.

Step #3:
When the period has ended, go to the child to discuss the problem in depth.
- ✓ Both parent and child will have had a chance to bring emotions under control.
- ✓ Utilize reflective listening and other communication skills (see chapter 13).
- ✓ If appropriate, use a problem-solving strategy (see chapter 5).
- ✓ Teach older children to come and confess their misdeed and ask for the parents' forgiveness.
- ✓ Mend feelings and reestablish a loving bond.

After the Time Out period, during the discussion that follows, encourage the child and share your confidence and expectations that the child's behavior will improve. This creates a very natural opportunity for a brief discussion of unacceptable impulses, and the importance of resisting temptations, etc. Some parents like to conclude the time with prayer before allowing the child to return to a previous or new activity.

THE ROD OF DISCIPLINE
Spanking is certainly an effective means of behavior control,

but it is not a remedy for every problem a child has. Remember, we said that punishment teaches what not to do, and spanking can do that very well, but it does not teach children the proper behavior for the next time they are faced with similar circumstances.

Scripture makes a strong case for spanking. For instance, Proverbs 13:24 says, "He who spares the rod hates his son, but he who loves him is careful to discipline him." Again, Proverbs 22:15 says, "Folly is bound up in the heart of a child, but the rod of discipline will drive it far from him."

The weakness found in spanking as a method of discipline involves knowing when and when not to use it as a tool. Some advocate spanking for every infraction regardless of the extent of the "crime" or the age of the child. This constitutes punishing constantly, ignores the need for nurture, and fails to acknowledge the differences in age-appropriate discipline. If a parent is given to punishing in anger, the danger exists that spanking may become abusive.

In order to decide if spanking is an appropriate tool to use in a specific situation, we suggest that you ask yourself the following questions:

√ Is the undesirable behavior an act of willful disobedience?

√ Was the correction a consistent consequence for the undesirable behavior?

√ Are you correcting the "deed" or the "doer"?

√ Does the spanking provoke your child's wrath?

√ What is your emotional state at the time of administering the spanking? If you are angry, the child may reason that the spanking is a function of your emotional state rather than the inherent wrongness of the misbehavior.

√ How would your child answer this question: Why did you get a spanking?

a. Because I made my parent angry.

b. Because I misbehaved (broke a rule, etc.).

If you decide to spank, should you use your hand or another object? Those who advocate using objects emphasize that the hand is to be used for caressing, loving, and nurturing. It is not to administer pain. However, those who say to use only the hand emphasize the increased risk of physical abuse and bodily harm when another object is used. We believe that what you use is not as important as the spirit in which you use it. If you choose to spank, be sure it is not done in anger.

GET IT DONE

The immediacy of correction, particularly with younger children, increases its effectiveness by directly linking it with the memory of the misbehavior. Ecclesiastes 8:11 tells us, "When the sentence for a crime is not quickly carried out, the hearts of the people are filled with schemes to do wrong." Remember, the key to any discipline method is consistency and immediacy.

The following chapters will add more tools to your toolbox, as well as give insight into some special family situations.

PART TWO

"I will show you what he is like who comes to Me and hears My words and puts them into practice. He is like a man building a house, who dug down deep and laid the foundation on rock. When a flood came, the torrent struck that house but could not shake it, because it was well built."

Luke 6:47-48

CHAPTER NINE

THE ABSENT PARENT

In Scripture God sets forth the ideal of raising children in two-parent families. However, for reasons that are not always clear to us, God sometimes does not allow two parents to survive or remain in the home. Being a single parent is a great challenge, but God can and will provide the wisdom and strength needed for the task. God promises, in Psalm 68:5, that He will be "a Father to the fatherless, a Defender of widows."

DEFINING THE PROBLEM

Divorce and death are two circumstances which bring about single-parent families. In some single-parent families, however, there has never been another parent. In others, the absent parent may still reside in the home but underfunction in the role of parent, making the other spouse for all intents and purposes a single parent.

Regardless of the initial situation which brought about the single-parent family, each of these families face similar obstacles. Grief over the loss of a parent in the home affects both parents and children, with anger and depression often accompanying the grief. The children must deal with insecurity, and the remaining parent may face feelings of inadequacy and resentment while attempting to do the work of two. The issue of resentment may be a particular problem when one partner underfunctions yet remains in the home.

WHAT GOES WRONG

Each single-parent family has a different story to tell about the circumstances leading up to their particular situation. However, most single-parent families face difficulties in bringing structure and discipline to the new family status. In our experience as family therapists, we have seen several repetitive patterns emerge in single-parent families.

PARENTS WITHOUT PARTNERS

Single parents typically respond to their children with a general loosening of rules and roles. Children who are grieving and facing the insecurity of a broken family need the stability of roles and rules more than ever. At the same time, parents who are grieving over a lost spouse or a broken marriage have the most difficulty in providing that structure. This may happen because of sympathy for the grief and insecurity the children have experienced in losing a parent. It may also take place because the single parent experiences loss and can't cope with all the changes that are occuring.

This lessening of rules and consequences tends to move the family into the chaotic area on the circumplex. At the same time, single parents may be tempted to deal with their own grief by confiding in their children and looking to their children as the primary source of emotional support. When this happens the family moves toward enmeshment.

PARENTS WITH JUNIOR PARTNERS

This pattern toward chaos and enmeshment commonly results in the elevation of children into parental roles. Children then begin to carry emotional loads that are not age appropriate for them by becoming a parent's best friend, or a parent's confidant. This establishes an unhealthy emotional bond between the parent and child, but to the parent it *feels* perfectly normal. The boundary around the parental child and parent may prove difficult to enter in the event of remarriage. Figure

19 shows a before and after genogram structure of a family when a parental child role develops.

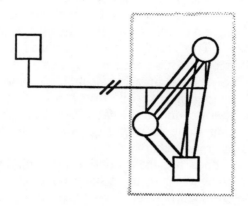

Figure 19. Genogram Showing Development of Parental Child After Divorce

PARENTS WITH TOO MANY PARTNERS

Generally, there is less supervision of children in a single-parent household. Parents who must work outside the home find it difficult to provide structure simply because there is less time to be with the children. Authority may need to be delegated to third parties — day care centers, teachers, coaches, scouting leaders, baby-sitters, etc. The minimal time left to parent leaves single parents with too little influence in the lives of their children. Consequently, children often are promoted to a higher level of independence before they are emotionally ready.

When single parents confide in their extended families, rather than in their children or a support group, the families tend to become overinvolved with the children. If the single parent underfunctions as a parent, grandparents or other relatives may step in and violate the family boundary by overfunctioning in the role of the absent partner. Sometimes, a boyfriend or girlfriend steps into the role of the missing parent. This intrudes on the sanctity of the nuclear family and fails to preserve the executive authority of the single parent.

PARENTS WITH UNDERFUNCTIONING PARTNERS
When the "absent" partner is an underfunctioning parent
who still lives in the home, the functioning parent often
teaches codependent behavior to their children. *Codependence* can be defined as "living with the disease, or the symptoms of disease." The family system stabilizes around the
symptom and adapts to it so that the dysfunction begins to
feel normal. The disease may be alcoholism, workaholism,
emotional disengagement, or any kind of addiction.
Codependents operate under the false belief that you must
leave the symptom alone or it will get worse, or they deny
that the symptom even exists.

Codependency does not exist outside of a relationship; it
does not describe who I am, but what I do in that relationship. The problem does not reside in a person's personality,
but in the choices they make within any relationship with a
person who displays dysfunctional patterns. When a person
learns to function as a codependent in one relationship, the
possibility exists that he or she will attempt to carry out the
same codependent behavior in all subsequent relationships.

If one parent's behavior enables the spouse to underfunction in order to keep "peace" in the family, the children will
learn to function the same way. When a codependent single
parent allows a child to overfunction as a parental child, that
parent also is unknowingly teaching a form of codependency
that will follow the child into adulthood.

Parents with underfunctioning partners have a tendency to
triangulate children into the marriage relationship. The overfunctioning parent forms a strong collusion with the children
and shuts the other parent out. Men who spend years
underfunctioning as fathers may find such a strong collusion
between Mom and the kids that it is impossible for him to get
back into the family. Figure 20 pictures this type of triangle.

PARENTS WITH GUILT
In chapter 7 we discussed reactive parenting: reacting to a
child's misbehavior rather than thinking ahead, responding to
circumstances and maintaining control of the child's behavior.

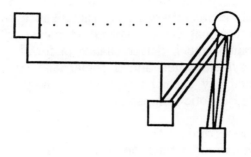

Figure 20. Parent-Child Collusion with Underfunctioning Father

Another form of reactive parenting involves reacting emotionally to family events and circumstances. The single parent becomes somewhat self-absorbed and preoccupied with her own emotions. She may find it difficult to think and act in the child's best interest. Parents may find themselves being overprotective of their children because of the grief and disruption they have experienced.

Reactive parenting also occurs when parents experience guilt over the breakup of a marriage. They protect the children from added responsibilities which should naturally occur with each new stage of growth. Because of the sympathy these parents feel for their children, they also tend to permit misbehavior which might not otherwise be allowed.

Anger can prevent parents from thinking through the overall picture of parenting: rules, consequences, how to solve problems with children, etc. The parents' emotions trigger their behavior. They then move into reactive parenting, allowing their emotions to dictate their behavior rather than following the basic principles for effective parenting.

BACK TO BASICS

It will probably come as no surprise that the principles of healthy single-parent family systems are the same as healthy two-parent family systems. For some single parents this may be the first opportunity they have had for putting some of the healthy family characteristics into place. Those who choose to do the emotional work involved in adjusting to single parenting stand a much better chance of forming a healthy new family system when and if remarriage occurs. Single parents should pay special attention to family structure in order to avoid chaotic enmeshment.

BALANCED PARENTING

When a two-parent family becomes a one-parent family, changes naturally occur in the family structure. But the changes don't have to devastate the emotional health of family members. It is imperative that the rules and consequences remain consistent—or be established if not previously in place. Children must know that the parent with whom they are living is in charge. This may prove difficult if the parent left with the children has never played a major role in establishing the rules and consequences. This parent must now take over and learn to do what he or she has never done before.

In order to maintain balance in the family structure, single parents will need a list of rules and consequences that are realistic for their situation. This list should be structured enough to provide the needed supervision of their children. As much as is possible, the family might be advised to restrict additional changes in lifestyle until children and parents have had time to adjust.

The grieving process tends to disrupt normal movement on the circumplex through the life cycle. Sometimes a need exists for a family to fall back and regroup—becoming a little more structured and connected in response to the crisis initially. But the time will come when normal progress must be resumed and parents must learn to let go. Figure 21 shows the ideal area on the circumplex for all families; the need for balance in both adaptability and cohesiveness cannot be stressed too much.

At no time should children be forced to choose between

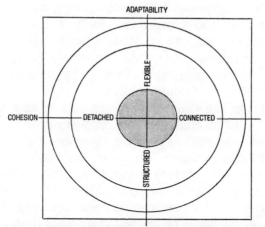

Figure 21. Circumplex Showing Ideal Balance Area for Well-functioning Families

their parents. When a parent criticizes another parent in the children's presence, it causes the children to make a choice between their parents. Children need opportunities to form opinions on their own and decide how they will relate to each parent.

LIMITED PARTNERSHIPS

The single parent is the executive in the family. Children do not benefit from being elevated to the role of a missing spouse. The oldest son does not become the "man of the house." He remains merely the oldest son with appropriate responsibilities for his age. Children can assume many chores around the house when a single parent is forced to work outside the home, but they should not have to supply emotional support for a parent.

It is best that parents avoid bringing their children into discussions about: finances, loneliness, concerns with the ex-spouse, court proceedings and settlements, terms of the divorce, or how the parents view each other. When parents draw children into these areas, looking to the child to meet these needs, the child crosses the executive boundary and becomes a parental child

If a parent expresses feelings of loneliness to a child, the parent needs to also express that he or she does not expect the child to fill that loneliness. If a parent tells a child that money is tight, he or she needs to reassure the child that the child need not worry about the money. Single parents need to take ownership for finding solutions to their problems without relying on the children to participate in that solution.

Close friends or members of a recovery group can support and nurture single parents, giving them an outlet for expressing worries and concerns. Children also need the support of friends and adults outside the family system. This type of support can prevent elevating children into parental roles, and can give children an avenue for expressing their needs without overwhelming an already grieving parent. Care needs to be taken, however, that these support people outside the nuclear family do not enter the family system and begin overfunctioning as surrogate parents.

Children of *all* ages need supervision while a single parent is at work. While this may put financial pressure on the single parent, the benefit of supervision and loving care of young children far outweighs any material deprivation they may suffer. With older children, parents need some say in who supervises the children. When anyone other than the parent cares for the children, the parent *delegates* authority to that person for nurture and discipline during the time the children are in the caregiver's care. Rules and consequences will need to be very specific and easily understood by anyone who is responsible for care-giving. In any caregiving situation—whether day care, school, baby-sitters, parents, in-laws, or church youth programs—parents still hold the God-given authority over their children's lives.

LEARNING INTERDEPENDENCE

Parents have the responsibility of helping their children to accept and adjust to the new situation of living with a single parent. Spending time individually with each child, being sensitive to the emotions the child experiences, and focusing on the positive aspects of the future facilitates this adjustment.

In this way, single parents and children can learn to be inter-dependent without violating boundaries.

A family system with an underfunctioning parent and spouse requires a special attitude on the part of the function-ing parent. We mentioned earlier the tendency in these fam-ilies to form collusional relationships between the active par-ent and the children against the underfunctioning parent. To avoid this, the active spouse must deal with any anger and resentment aimed toward the underfunctioner. Luke 6:27-42 and Matthew 18:15-17 offer help for those dealing with diffi-cult spouses.

A constant attitude of forgiveness, such as Jesus displayed, keeps resentment from building. This attitude of forgiveness makes it possible for the functioning parent to include the underfunctioning parent in family plans. Even if he or she doesn't follow through, the day may come when the desire develops for a relationship with the functioning spouse and children, and the door needs to be left open for that.

PARENTING WITHOUT GUILT
Unrecognized emotions and unresolved conflicts may in-crease reactive parenting. Parents and children must allow each other to complete the grieving process, without denying the hurt they have experienced. Feeling anger is a normal stage of grieving and must be faced, confessed, and talked about without defensiveness. As emotional healing takes place, parents will find themselves better able to respond to their children in love while maintaining the rules and struc-ture of the family. When parents establish their hierarchical position of authority, the tendency toward reactive parenting lessens.

Children pick up on conflict between parents whether mar-ried or divorced. Denying the truth or pretending that conflict doesn't exist teaches children to mistrust their own thoughts and feelings. Responsive parents insulate their children from the nitty-gritty details while not attempting to hide the fact that conflict exists. Children are quick to blame themselves for problems in the parents' relationship, so children need assurance that the marriage breakup or ongoing conflict is not their fault.

A HELPING HAND
Parents who face the task of parenting without a partner often need help in setting guidelines for their family situation. God recognized the special needs of families who have lost a father or a mate, and declared that He Himself would take that person's place. Single parents can find the emotional and physical strength they need by relying on the indwelling presence of God's Holy Spirit.

CHAPTER TEN

RECASTING
THE MOLD

Making the change from marriage to single parenting sometimes causes distress. Making the change from single-parent family to remarried family sometimes causes disaster. Healthy stepfamilies don't just happen. The family mold must be recast, and this requires time, patience, and hard work.

Families can count on the Lord for strength to do the hard work required, as well as His guidance and wisdom to deal with the problems that stepfamilies face. Though Scripture doesn't address the stepfamily specifically, 2 Corinthians 6:18 reminds us that, in a sense, we are all stepchildren: "I will be a Father to you, and you will be my sons and daughters, says the Lord Almighty."

DEFINING THE PROBLEM

The problems of bonding with stepchildren while trying to establish a new marriage often prove overwhelming for the new family. More than 75 percent of second marriages end in divorce. Our experience as family therapists suggests these marriages often fail to anticipate and to understand the dynamics involved in stepparenting.

When divorce was the reason for the single-parent situation, the first failed marriage can cause continued problems in the new marriage. Most stepfamilies contain at least one victim of an unhealthy family system and an unhealthy first marriage. Consequently, the new marriage does not begin with two emotionally well-functioning people, but with the remnants of dysfunctional systems. These two dysfunctional remnants come together and try to make one healthy, functional whole. The difficulty that two recovering unhealthy individuals face in making a marriage work should give some idea of the enormity of the task facing these two people when stepchildren are involved.

The task may be equally as difficult when the death of a spouse caused the single-parent state. The problems faced by each type of stepfamily are similar, with the possible exception of having to deal with a noncustodial parent.

WHAT GOES WRONG

As we stated in chapter 9, single-parent families tend to become more chaotic and enmeshed. If this has happened and has not been corrected before remarriage occurs, then the stepparent faces the challenge of joining a system with poorly defined roles and collusional boundaries.

DON'T FENCE ME OUT

Boundaries are like fences — some have gates, some don't. If a boundary without a gate was established around the single parent and children, the new stepparent may have a difficult time opening up that boundary and finding a place within it. When a chaotic family structure exists, the oldest child may have been put in a parental role. The remarriage of the natural parent means that this child will be "dethroned" — a position not given up easily by most children who have achieved it.

The enmeshment of the natural parents to their children forms a collusion and this tight boundary around them may shut out the new stepparent and create a triangle. When the stepparent attempts to discipline the children or assume a position of authority, the collusion between parent and child provokes anger against the stepparent. Eventually, many stepparents find themselves excluded from family affairs.

Codependent relationships in recast families occur when stepparents attempt to rescue or help their new partner whom they perceive as "weak." Many women who remarry fall innocently into the role of the weaker partner. If single parents have allowed the family structure to become chaotic, rules and consequences likely have not been enforced and the children probably are out of control.

Enter a loving stepparent anxious to restore some order in the family. This stepparent sees the new partner as a weak, ineffectual disciplinarian (which may be true) and attempts to take over the position of authority in the family. Because of reasons to be discussed in the next section, the stepparent does not yet have the right to do this and merely produces anger and rebellion in the children, which in turn arouses a spirit of overprotectiveness in the new mate.

Natural parents often use the defense of their children as a substitute for conflict resolution with their new partner. Lack of conflict resolution leads to serious consequences in a first marriage; in a remarriage the results are explosive. Failure to settle the issues of divided family loyalty, delegation of authority, and defining roles is like combining gasoline and a lighted match.

WRONGFUL ASSUMPTION OF AUTHORITY

God charges parents with the responsibility to take authority over their children. *Any authority a stepparent might have over the children must be delegated to them by the natural parent.* In order for natural parents to delegate authority, two things must happen. First, natural parents must have assumed their God-given authority and practiced it with the children. They can't delegate what they don't have. Second, they must be willing to share the role of parenting with the new stepparent. When stepparents become stronger in their discipline of the children than the natural parents, the children rebel and the natural parents instinctively protect the children. The stepparents have started a war they cannot win.

Headship and submission are difficult concepts to manage in first marriages. In remarriages, it becomes essential to understand these concepts in the context of Scripture. Headship is never a "ruling" position; it is a position of submission and service—it is relationship as well as leadership. Jesus demonstrated these characteristics over and over with His disciples. Misunderstanding the nature of a "head of the household" position can cause serious, and often fatal, damage to a stepparent family.

NONCUSTODIAL INTRUSION

Divorce doesn't end a relationship with the ex-spouse; it just redefines the roles, rules, and boundaries of that former relationship. The old system is not buried with divorce; it's alive and overflowing with visitation and custodial issues.

Many divorced, noncustodial parents handle their situation fairly well until their former spouse remarries. Now, with a new person in the picture trying to build a relationship with their children and former spouse, noncustodial parents find feelings of rejection, hostility, jealousy, and anger emerging. They must face the pain of knowing that their children are now with another parent. Most noncustodial parents have no prior life experience to help them in knowing how to manage these unfamiliar feelings.

Men especially suffer from the feelings of grief and hostility at their children being removed one more step from them. It's not unusual for noncustodial parents to file motions to modify custody. Many make attempts at reconciliation with their former spouse when they learn of an impending remarriage. Failing this, the noncustodial parent may begin to express grief and to make critical remarks about the new stepparent to the children. There may be a sincere attempt on the part of noncustodial parents to improve relationships with their children. This, in turn, causes guilt and confusion in the children, who may come to feel that the only way to protect their natural parent is to shut out the stepparent.

To make matters even more complicated, the children are facing a new loss of their own: the loss of the fantasy that Mom and Dad will someday make up and the family will be together again. This loss is very real to the children, and the grief process they go through needs to be recognized and facilitated by both natural parent and stepparent. During the time of adjusting to the new marriage, children may feel abandoned by the natural parent. The grief and loss may cause children to misbehave and act out when they otherwise would not.

Children react in similar ways when the noncustodial parent remarries first. In addition, when noncustodial parents remarry, their interest becomes divided between the children of the previous marriage and their new spouse. Because of this, time spent in visitation is often reduced, leaving the children to cope with feelings of rejection.

BACK TO BASICS

The problems faced by stepparent families may seem overwhelming, but the answer, once again, is to carefully and consistently apply the basic principles for healthy family functioning. This often requires "unlearning" certain behaviors and attitudes before new ones can be established in their place. For stepparent families, it is essential that both husband and wife step back and take a look at the strengths and weaknesses of their first family in order to learn how to make the stepparent family healthy. The process of reconstituting a family may take one to two years, with slowly increasing signs of peace and security within the family.

In working with many hundreds of stepfamilies, we have discovered the following principles:

FAMILY STRUCTURE

Parents and children must first open their boundaries and allow the stepparent (and any stepsiblings) into the family system. The parents must then redefine the roles that each person in the family will assume. In order to do this, the parents will have to clearly communicate their intentions and expectations and resolve conflicts as they begin to emerge.

It is absolutely vital that both the natural parent and the stepparent be in agreement about the rules and consequences and speak with one voice in disciplinary matters. In the beginning, however, the primary task of the stepparent is to form a bond with each stepchild. This requires a commitment to building as intimate a relationship with the stepchildren as possible. This includes learning to handle the grief, disappointment, and anger that the stepchildren may misdirect toward the stepparent.

Ephesians 6:4 instructs us to avoid provoking our children's anger by making sure that punishment occurs within a loving and nurturing relationship. Stepparents have a lot of catching up to do in nurturing the children. Until a loving bond has been established, the stepparent must assume the role primarily of a nurturer, supporting the natural parent as the disciplinarian.

Most stepparents, see behaviors in their stepchildren that concern them. However, stepparents need to refrain from reacting, exercise patience, and work on nurturing the relationship with both their spouse and the children. They can talk to their partner about the needs that they see in the children and let the natural parent take the lead in setting limits and enforcing consequences. In the meantime, the stepparent can look for ways to eliminate obstacles to a relationship with the children and create opportunities for building intimacy. They can give positive reinforcement to the children, their individual abilities, and achievements.

It takes time for the stepparent and natural parent to develop trust and intimacy in their own relationship, as well as find a balance in their differing styles of parenting. Until these marital tasks have been accomplished, it's very unlikely that the stepparent's efforts at influencing the stepchildren's behavior will be successful.

GAINING A POSITION OF AUTHORITY
Parental authority is given by God to a biological parent. A stepparent's authority is delegated by the natural parent, not by God. As the bond between stepparent and stepchild grows, so does the effectiveness of using that delegated authority.

When the natural parent has not exercised authority with the children, then that situation must be corrected before any authority can be delegated to the stepparent. It is important for the natural parent and stepparent to arrive at a mutually agreeable set of rules and consequences. Then, the natural parent must take the lead in putting those rules and consequences into effect. The stepparent's role must initially be to support and affirm the natural parent's actions.

If the natural parent has a system of rules and consequences in place, then the sharing of authority begins with the two parents defining the roles they will play in the family. If the stepparent disagrees with the way the natural parent disciplines the children, then the two parents should negotiate the rules and consequences to be enforced. This is an opportunity for the two parents to learn how to blend their differing styles of parenting.

If the parents negotiate the rules and consequences in front of the children, they must be careful to successfully resolve this conflict. Otherwise, they empower the children to play one parent against the other. As the children experience the parent and stepparent respectfully negotiating—speaking openly from their hearts, listening carefully to each other, coming to a mutually agreeable decision—they will learn how to resolve conflicts with each other.

MAKING ROOM FOR NONCUSTODIAL PARENTS

A custodial parent can relieve a lot of tension by fostering a close relationship between the children and the noncustodial parent. Recognition of the grief that a noncustodial parent faces when a former spouse remarries can help the stepfamily cope with the part this "outsider" now plays in the new family situation.

Healthy families have boundaries. Even though there is a noncustodial parent who has visitation rights with the children, the family boundaries need not be violated. If the children come back from a visit with the noncustodial parent and begin to misbehave or show disrespect toward either parent, the situation should be dealt with calmly and lovingly. The stepparent and natural parent *together* define what is inappropriate behavior for the custodial household and set realistic consequences if the misbehavior continues. It is best to not blame, attack, or make critical remarks about the noncustodial parent. To do so puts the children in the position of defending the noncustodial parent, and takes the focus off their misbehavior.

When a parent remarries, children need reassurance that this new marriage will not hinder their relationship with their natural, noncustodial parent. It is in the best interest of the child for the custodial parent to foster a healthy relationship between the child and the noncustodial parent. Only damage comes from undermining this relationship.

The best thing the noncustodial parent can do for his or her children is to foster a healthy bonding with the new stepparent. Noncustodial parents need to recognize and deal with the grief of another person becoming a nurturing caregiver to their children. Noncustodial parents can reduce the sense of divided loyalty or betrayal by permitting and encouraging their children to refer to the stepparent by whatever title the children choose. (Noncustodial parents might also suggest acceptable titles.) They should stay out of a hostile relationship with the stepparent, as much as it might hurt to see their children loving someone else. They do their children a great disservice if they attempt to draw their children's loyalty away from the stepfamily.

The only time it is ever in a child's best interest to have no contact with a noncustodial parent is when there is verifiable abuse. Even then, it may be therapeutic, when safety can be assured, for the child to confront the abuse issue and forgive the abusing parent. Our experience is that this is best accomplished under the supervision of a competent family therapist.

MEETING THE CHALLENGE
The tasks and obstacles that stepfamilies face may seem overwhelming. However, healthy stepfamilies are built on the same principles as any other well-functioning family: clear roles, specific rules, and consistently applied consequences. Add patience and a sense of humor and the rewards of a happy, secure family will make all the effort worthwhile.

CHAPTER ELEVEN

SCHOOL DAZE

Some children breeze through school without causing as much as a ripple on the sea of family life. Others, it seems, carry hurricane-strength turbulence with them as they attack the patience of both the school and the family systems. Many reasons exist for differences in learning capacity and compliance in children. We often reach adulthood before grasping the truth of Proverbs 2:10-11: "For wisdom will enter your heart, and knowledge will be pleasant to your soul. Discretion will protect you, and understanding will guard you."

DEFINING THE PROBLEM

Five-year-old children preparing to start kindergarten vary in a multitude of ways. By temperament, a child may be shy and timid, quiet and serious, loud and rambunctious, or a million other variations on these themes. How well children do in a structured classroom setting depends to a great extent on how well they can bring their natural temperament into line with the school's expectations for them.

Maturity levels also differ greatly in children of school age. A level of physical maturity is needed for the tasks required of school children as they move from grade to grade. Mental and emotional maturity play a part in a child's readiness to learn and to conform to the school's standards of behavior.

A child's motivation for learning depends to a large extent on the parents. If they are excited about their child attending school and remain interested in his progress, then the child stands a greater chance of maintaining his motivation for learning. Parents who display an indifference to their children's school experiences often pass that emotion on to their children. No amount of lectures on studying will make up for the parents' general lack of interest.

Parents may show genuine interest in their children's progress in school, and yet fail to make it a priority in family scheduling. Many outside activities compete for the time of both parents and children. Keeping priorities balanced may become difficult for over-involved families.

WHAT GOES WRONG

With so many factors playing a part in a child's adjustment to school, it becomes difficult to pinpoint exact causes for poor performance. No matter what the particular problem a child may experience, each area—family, school, temperament, maturity, motivation, and a child's choices—must be examined for the part it plays in the situation.

ATTENTION DEFICIT DISORDER AND HYPERACTIVITY

Many children have difficulty adapting to a structured classroom situation because of physical, emotional, or mental immaturity. Unfortunately, many of these children get labeled as problem children, and that label follows them throughout their school years.

Today, hyperactive behavior is best understood as a symptom that occurs in some children who also suffer from a difficulty in focusing and sustaining their attention. This is referred to as Attention Deficit Disorder (A.D.D.). The terms A.D.D. and A.D.H.D. are used to identify children with attention difficulties without and with hyperactive behavior. In addition, A.D.D. and A.D.H.D. children may also have other specific learning disabilities. The true A.D.H.D. child is believed to have a mild neurological disorder, once previously called M.B.D. (Minimal Brain Dysfunction).

Children diagnosed as A.D.H.D. not only have trouble focusing their attention, but also find it hard to control or modify their behavior to fit the environment. Most children realize that the loud, rowdy behavior tolerated in gym class becomes inappropriate in the library, but the A.D.H.D. child cannot change his behavior as the situation changes.

There is no definitive test to determine the presence of A.D.D. or A.D.H.D. in a child. The label is a subjective one that may or may not help clarify the problem. It doesn't necessarily explain the cause or point at any particular solution. Parents should be cautious about allowing such a designation to be attached to their child.

A.D.D. and A.D.H.D. are not diseases. Often the diagnosis is based upon the child's "nuisance value." That is, it is based more on the level of tolerance adults have than on the severity of symptoms. The environment the child is in, and the tolerance of the adults present in that environment, determine the boundaries of the nuisance value.

Many of these same children who have difficulty learning in a formal classroom setting have mastered the English language and many other feats of knowledge before entering school. Most of the children *do not* have an impairment in learning; they have an impairment in learning *under the specific circumstances* in which the school places them.

Many children who are labeled as hyperactive are really hyper reactive to the problems in their family system. Children often suffer from a lack of self-control because they feel anxiety due to a dysfunctional family system. That is, they express through their behavior the chaos in their home life.

We will have more to say about the treatment of A.D.D. and A.D.H.D. in the "Back To Basics" section of this chapter.

THE UNDERACHIEVER

A child is considered to be an underachiever when his performance falls below the *expected* level of achievement. This happens for a variety of reasons. Sometimes children have not developed the self-discipline they need, or they may be unmotivated. Some children may suffer from an actual learning impairment and need tutoring. In other cases, parents' or teachers' expectations are higher than the child's ability.

Some children develop early and parents may make the false inference that early learning means high intelligence. Other children may function very well in a certain area, and their parents may believe this means the child will be able to function just as well in every area. Some parents are incorrectly led to believe by professionals that their child has a high level of functioning.

Parents must first assess the belief that the child supposedly could be functioning at a higher level but isn't. There are definitive tests to indicate whether or not a child really is an underachiever. On standardized tests, if it is professionally determined that the child has aptitudes that are not reflected in grades and classroom work, the child is considered an underachiever. However, this does not explain the underlying cause of the underachievement.

Parents with a child who consistently works below his level of ability may find that they are unintentionally reinforcing the child's behavior in some way. To change the child's behavior, parents need to determine what is reinforcing the underachievement. What is the child getting out of it? It may seem to the parent that the child is receiving only punishment, but negative attention is still attention and meets a need in the child. The parents and child may find themselves trapped in a vicious cycle of underachievement and negative attention.

THE HOMEWORK BLUES
Perhaps the most common type of school-related problem relates to homework. Children often neglect to do assigned homework tasks at home. Sometimes the work is done, but the child consistently fails to turn it in on time—or at all. Many children rush through homework, and therefore do a sloppy job of it, in order to get at another, more favored activity.

Children often need a little extra help in understanding what is expected of them. Some parents require their children to do their homework with no supervision, whether or not the children are capable of working on their own. On the other side of the homework dilemma, some parents become too involved in their children's homework and do the work for them. If you find yourself asking your child, "How did we do on our homework today?" you may be guilty of homework enmeshment! When a parent becomes responsible for making sure the assignment is finished, or becomes more concerned about deadlines than the student, then a codependent relationship exists. The Science Fair is an excellent place to detect codependency.

Parents can require too much at one time from children with a very short attention span. Timid children are often confused and made even more shy by high, unrealistic expectations and demands. On the other hand, when nonassertive parents yield to unruly children, the children's behavior, and consequently the quality of their work, can quickly become out of control.

LACK OF STRUCTURE

Most of the problems with homework develop because of a lack of family structure. Any of the extreme positions on the circumplex brings with it a set of problems that will interfere with good homework and study skills. Chaotic families may fail to make time for homework; rigid families may damage their children's progress in school by excessive or unrealistic expectations and demands. Disengaged families tend to not give enough support to the child when help is needed with schoolwork; enmeshed families, as we've already mentioned, often do the work for the child.

EDUCATIONAL TRIANGLES

Parents often get caught in the trap of siding with their children in a collusion against teachers, schools, and other professionals. This establishes a triangle and tends to foster an attitude of defiance on the part of the children. Triangles are always unhealthy and that includes when they occur with others outside the family system.

BACK TO BASICS

A key principle for any parent of school-age children to remember is that the education belongs to the child, not the parents. Parents have had their chance in the past and nothing the child does, or doesn't do, will change the parents' own school experience. While school occupies a high priority in a child's life, it is not the top priority. Establishing a balance between family time, leisure, exercise, spiritual growth activities, and social development is of even greater importance.

Family life must go on; when a child's school difficulties become the primary focus, little room exists for family time. Parents need to set some basic guidelines and structure the family in a way that will encourage each child to do his best. But parents should not demand perfection of their children, or allow children to demand it of themselves.

TREATING ATTENTION DEFICIT DISORDER AND HYPERACTIVITY
Parents whose children have been diagnosed with either A.D.D. or A.D.H.D. need to remember that their task in the home is the same as any other family: Apply the basic principles of a healthy family system. True A.D.D. and A.D.H.D. children, as well as those who are misdiagnosed, benefit from structure and consistency.

Generally, three options exist for the treatment of A.D.D. and A.D.H.D. The treatments may be cominbed but *all* of these options require professional input and help. The first mode of treatment involves modifying the child's environment with the assistance of a family therapist. This treatment requires looking for any dysfunction in the family system, and working for a balanced family style on the circumplex.

The A.D.D. child needs structure with clear limits and consequences. The child's life should include a balance of activities: homework time, leisure time, family time. The parents can assist with schoolwork if the child needs help, but should also expect their child to work independently when capable. In order to accomplish this, the parents will need regular feedback from the school in order to know what the child should be working on at home.

The second option, behavior modification, trains the child to develop behavioral controls. The professional family therapist can help the family develop specific strategies, exercises, and assignments for modifying the rules and consequences within the home environment. Applying these techniques will enable the child to develop internal behavioral controls.

The final option uses medication to subdue a child's behavior and bring it under control. For children who have some neurologically based difficulty, this may be a wise alternative. However, some children respond to treatment by medication—implying a neurological cause—even when the root of their problem resides in the family system rather than in their neurological system.

Medication is the easiest and most frequently used approach to treatment of A.D.D. and A.D.H.D. children, even when it may not be necessary. *We believe that medication alone is seldom, if ever, appropriate for these children.* Even when medication is being considered, family involvement and behavior modification techniques must also coexist.

Many parents are concerned about the effect that taking medication will have on the child's resistance to abusing drugs later on. The prescription itself should not be considered harmful; however, when parents choose the easy route of relying solely on medication, children learn to look upon drugs as a solution to life's problems. Even when medication is used, children must learn that they can't rely on the pill to solve problems for them. Children must develop new strategies for sitting still and for maintaining attention.

We believe that if parents try the options of environment and behavior modification first, they may find it unnecessary to use medication. In some extreme cases, however, environment and behavior modification will not be enough, and it may actually be harmful to the child not to medicate. We have found that when all the options for treatment are used in conjunction with each other, the dosage level of the medication will be smaller than with medication alone. The length of time needed for medication treatment may be shortened also.

The preferred treatment for hyperactive and hyper reactive

children, especially those who suffer no verifiable neurological impairment, is the application of basic family system principles: structure, consistency, and involvement. Parents must find the best match between increasing or decreasing the stimulation, length of study periods, and individual vs. group learning activities. The key is to balance the demands of the environment and the needs of the child. This is best done by the parents and the child in cooperation with the family therapist, physician, and the child's teacher. Treating A.D.D. and A.D.H.D. is a team effort.

HEALTHY FAMILY STRUCTURE

Families who struggle with homework problems, as well as those who face hyperactivity and attention deficit disorders, can solve many of their school-related problems by following the guidelines for a healthy family system.

Schools, in a sense, are stepparents for a few hours a day, and therefore have only the authority delegated to them by the parents of the children they teach. Parents should never give over all authority for teaching children to the schools. At all times, parents need to be involved in their children's schools. They should get to know the teachers and those in authority over the schools and keep an eye on what is being taught to their children.

One dangerous concept that some school systems teach is that children will naturally outgrow irresponsibility. Children will outgrow a certain amount of immaturity, but responsibility must be taught. It does not come automatically.

Healthy families share certain characteristics. These loving, caring families share time together and express affection toward each other. They set clear rules for their children, with appropriate consequences when children break those rules. Some of these rules have to do with homework but the effects of them will carry over into the classroom.

PARENT-SCHOOL INVOLVEMENT

Parents can avoid becoming triangulated with their children and a teacher or school by keeping two-way communication open between each element of the system. This keeps the parents empowered as the authority over their children's school experience, without delegating too much authority to the school and the children.

Parents can authorize the schools to teach academics to their children, but when it comes to dealing with values, motivation, and self-discipline, that's still the parents' responsibility. Children need to see their parents studying, whether they are trying to improve their skills for work, or doing personal Bible study. Children who see their parents investing time in improving their minds and getting a better education are going to be more inclined to want to study. Parents have to value education in their own lives, and strive for excellence in the things that they do — that's a healthy role model and a strong motivator.

The school becomes the parents' helpmate in educating their children. Parents must continue to remain involved in their children's overall equipping to function as adults. Learn as much as you can about your children's teachers and how they structure the classroom, and the teachers' expectations for your children. Do this by conversing with your children and by visiting the school often. If a problem develops, make sure to communicate with everyone involved, and refuse to get trapped in a triangle.

CURING THE HOMEWORK BLUES
Homework involves three steps: assignments, review, and interaction with parents. These steps change somewhat as the child develops, but the need for all three remains the same. Preschool, kindergarten, and elementary school-age children will spend more time interacting with parents about their day and less time on assignments. This time of interaction can become a family sharing activity, and can help establish in the child's mind that the parents are the authority over school as well as home. These sharing times should be relaxed and fun for everyone — letting the child teach the family a song she has learned, or tell a story he's heard. It is not just a time of review, but also a time of family closeness.

As children progress through school, they have more frequent homework assignments. At first, parents may need to supervise a child's study time closely, making sure that assignments are done neatly and completely. This supervision should gradually cease as the child demonstrates responsibility in this area. If at any time the child should fail to complete his assignments, then the parents can return to more direct supervision for a while.

One aspect of homework that is frequently overlooked involves reviewing the work done in class that day. Even if a child has no homework assignment, there is still homework to do. Chapters, notes, and previous tests all can be reviewed for a specified amount of time in the evening. We believe that children should spend a certain amount of time each night working on their education whether or not they have specific assignments. The amount of time differs for each child according to age and ability. Once again, this affirms that the parents are the primary educators in their children's lives, not the school.

As with assignments, the parents' involvement with review will lessen as children grow. For teenagers, the review will be more self-directed and will not involve as much family sharing time. However, parents should still be interacting about the school day with their teenagers.

Parents need periodic reports from their children's teachers, not just at nine-week intervals. By talking with teachers, parents can see if the information they get from their children coincides with the actual happenings in the classroom. When there is a problem with school performance, it's essential that parents get regular reports from the teachers, on a daily basis if the problem is severe. When the child begins to exercise increasing responsibility in the classroom, these reports can decrease in frequency.

Structure and consistency are important in establishing good homework skills. In general:

✓ Have a set time and place for homework to be done each day, as well as times for other important family functions.

√ Set learning goals with each child for the school year and work with them to help them achieve those goals.

√ Establish the study habit by asking, "What do you need to study tonight?" rather than "Do you have any homework?"

√ Parents should check homework for accuracy and neatness until the child has demonstrated reliability in this area.

√ Parents should properly assess the attention span of each child, and structure study time to be slightly less than that.

√ Begin with a young, or timid child, by supervising study time and offering help and encouragement with lessons. As the child matures and demonstrates reliability, spend less time in direct supervision.

A WORK ABOUT HOME SCHOOLING

Parents who opt to home-school their children need to be aware of the characteristics of a healthy system. Dysfunctional families that attempt to home-school create an unhealthy learning environment for their children. Healthy learning environments, like healthy families, have structure, boundaries, and clear rules and consequences. Families that home-school may find that they have an even greater responsibility to provide structure than families that send their children to public schools.

There needs to be a set time for schoolwork. It should be the same time every day, and nothing should be allowed to interfere with this time. Some families who home-school may fall into the trap of drilling their children over the course of a day. There must be a boundary between school time and time for other family activities. As Ecclesiastes 3:1-8 says, there is a time for everything. Children need time to be children.

Parents who home-school, or are thinking about it, should ask themselves some basic questions: Do we have a healthy family system in place? Am I able to separate family time from school time? Do I have the gift of teaching—especially my own children? Am I long-suffering and patient with my children? Do my children have exposure to other adults and children outside of the family boundaries, or is home schooling a way to keep them isolated?

CHILD GUIDANCE
First Thessalonians 5:14 offers some guidance we believe transfers well to parents of school-age children: "And we urge you, brothers, warn those who are idle, encourage the timid, help the weak, be patient with everyone." Lazy children should be warned, and clear consequences should follow if they fail to do their work. Timid children, those with poor self-esteem and low frustration levels, should be gently encouraged and guided until they develop the self-confidence necessary to do the work on their own. Weak children need help in understanding their work, and perhaps tutoring after school. And don't forget the final word of advice in the verse: Be patient with everyone. Anger serves no purpose in gaining control over school problems.

CHAPTER TWELVE

AVOIDING THE BIG TALK

Training up a child in the way he or she should go includes teaching healthy Christian sexuality. Contrary to what a lot of people would have you believe, those words are not contradictory terms. When Adam and Eve lost the ability to be "naked and unashamed" because of sin, healthy sexuality was hidden behind fear and inhibition. However, God does not hide His eyes or mince words when it comes to sexuality. Instead, He offers some very straightforward teaching in His Word.

Once parents understand for themselves what healthy sexuality means, they can be straightforward in teaching their children as well, following the instruction found in Deuteronomy 6:7: "Impress them [these commandments] on your children. Talk about them when you sit at home and when you walk along the road, when you lie down and when you get up."

DEFINING THE PROBLEM
The question of when and how to teach children about sex and sexuality frightens most parents. Parents who feel uncomfortable with their own sexual feelings struggle even more with the issue. These parents generally end up doing one of two things: They manage to avoid the subject altogeth-

er, or the teaching they give is limited and laced with harsh, stringent warnings. Other parents tend to dump all the information about sex at the first hint of a question and overwhelm children with more than they can appropriately understand.

WHAT GOES WRONG

Avoidance is the most common way parents handle teaching their children about sexuality. Through their silence, parents delegate sex education to the schools or leave it to the children's peers. Avoidance produces inhibitions on the part of both parents and children, and children come to believe that it is unacceptable to discuss such topics with their parents. By failing to discuss adult sexuality as something desirable and pleasurable, parents clearly communicate the message that it is either undesirable and unpleasant, or a very bad subject. Children then turn to peers for information. Consequently, children end up with a lot of misinformation and a humanistic notion of what is and isn't acceptable sexual behavior.

Because of the AIDS epidemic, public schools feel an urgency to present sex information to children at a much younger age than would have been the norm a few years ago. But schools fail to teach morality and decision-making along with sex education. Research confirms that schools involved in teaching sex education have a marked increase in sexual activity and abortions among the students. Parents, therefore, have an increased responsibility to do the foundational work in teaching about biblical sexuality before the schools teach about sex.

The church, unfortunately, hasn't offered much help to parents in this area. At church, children learn what not to do with their sexual curiosity—if they learn anything at all. Some children are never exposed to a healthy, positive attitude about sexuality. They need this type of attitude modeled for them, coupled with solid biblical teaching on Christian morals.

Children are becoming sexually active at younger and

younger ages. This happens because of: more freedom to car date at earlier ages, a lack of chaperoned activities, the influence of movies and TV shows which glorify sexual immorality and sexual pleasure outside of marriage, and of course, peer pressure. Many parents, even Christian ones, see this as inevitable and don't even make an attempt at teaching the notion of abstinence until marriage.

A parent's lack of understanding of the difference between sex and sexuality fosters the "Big Talk" method of sex education. The belief that one conversation can encompass the whole of sex education is possibly the biggest hindrance to properly teaching children about sexuality.

BACK TO BASICS

Sexuality has to do with maleness, femaleness, and the nature of relationships between males and females. Parents teach this, whether they try or not, by the roles they assume in the family and the husband-wife relationship they model. The children learn to respond to the opposite sex in the same way as their mother and father respond to each other. Therefore, *teaching healthy sexuality starts with having a healthy executive subsystem that properly models emotional intimacy.* For instance, children learn a lesson about intimacy when they see their parents go off on a Friday night date while they stay with a baby-sitter.

The act of sex is only one small part—though a very special part—of emotional intimacy within a marriage. Husbands and wives who want to deepen their emotional intimacy treat each other with respect and mutual submission, and do things that please each other. Parents should also model modesty and privacy to their children by placing limits and boundaries around the marriage relationship. Those limits and boundaries include keeping children out of the parents' bed, and teaching that there are times when children do not violate a closed bedroom door.

Parents need to focus on teaching sexuality education instead of sex education. When we teach about the nature of healthy relationships, Christian morality, and biblical limits, then talking about the act of sex is not as intimidating or scary. Parents make the same mistake that the schools make when they teach sex without first establishing a foundation for appropriate and healthy relationships. For those parents who feel they need some education themselves in this area, check the bibliography.

Teaching children about adult sexuality is a process, not an event. Included in this process are such things as giving age-appropriate information about sexuality and sex as a child grows. Sexuality education is part of the process talked about in Deuteronomy 6:7. Speaking to our children about sexuality should be as natural as walking and talking.

Molestation happens more frequently than we want to believe, even to good children in Christian families. Parents need to teach their young children about "good touch" and "bad touch." Open, honest communication will allow children to talk to parents about anyone who may have tried to touch them in an inappropriate way.

We believe that Christian parents can raise their children to be sexually abstinent until marriage. Children who understand the true nature of intimacy and all that is required of a lasting relationship stand a better chance of remaining abstinent. They need an understanding of their bodies, and a healthy dose of self-respect. They also need encouragement and wise guidance from their parents. This includes setting reasonable guidelines for dating both with and without supervision. Boys need these guidelines as much as girls.

Parents can offer alternatives to car dating until a child reaches an agreed upon age; they can encourage young teens to date in groups. Parents can make sure that teens go to activities that are properly supervised, and set limits on movie attendance and the type of movies that may be seen. Make sure teens have clear objectives for a date and know where they are going, with whom, and the curfew.

A BALANCED LIFE

Dating is part of a balanced Christian life that also includes: friends of the same sex, leisure time, spiritual development, worship, homework, sports, music, family time, and a host of other things. Emotional intimacy with parents, siblings, extended family, and same-sex friends is a good hedge against early sexual behavior. Preoccupation with a single person of the opposite sex to the exclusion of other people and activities is unacceptable. Parents may need to assert their authority to ensure that their children have balanced lives.

CHAPTER THIRTEEN

HEARING AIDS

God must have known how much trouble men and women would have communicating with one another. His Word, especially the Book of Proverbs, contains reference after reference on the use and misuse of the tongue. In Proverbs 16:23, God shares the secret of good communication: "A wise man's heart guides his mouth, and his lips promote instruction."

DEFINING THE PROBLEM

As a general rule, most of us approach the task of communication with three misconceptions. One involves the expectation that others are mind-readers and should somehow discern what we mean even if we don't give all the necessary information. Another misconception concerns the notion that when I say a word, everyone within my hearing will understand that word the way I do. The third misconception is that others will agree with me and with my opinions. However, God did not give any of us the ability to read one another's mind. In addition, even the simplest word can mean many different things to different people, and this makes disagreement a daily occurrence in most families. The attitudes behind the words we use can convey messages that the words themselves do not. Body language and tone of voice tell much about the true meaning behind our words. A simple sentence such as, "Honey, I don't mind if you go fishing," may be given a number of interpretations by the way it is spoken and the look in the eyes of the speaker. Words can be used as clubs to wound another person, or to "put them in their place." Parents often injure the fragile self-esteem of their children with criticism and sarcasm. Children, especially when raised in a critical environment, learn quickly how to hurt parents with a few choice words.

WHAT GOES WRONG

Miscommunication can sometimes resemble a comedy routine. One mother remarked that she often wondered if she and her son were having the same conversation. This can happen when two people don't take the time to see if they understand the words each is using.

Parents damage their ability to communicate when they show disrespect to each other or their children, and allow their children to do the same. When parents argue endlessly and never resolve the issues, they demonstrate poor communication to their children. Instead of good communication skills and healthy conflict resolution, these parents teach their children bad habits. Whining, yelling, crying, lack of eye contact, and disrespect replace shared feelings and ideas.

Some parents have a tendency to be disrespectful when their children are talking. They interrupt their children, finish their sentences, or correct their grammar. Parents often fail to make eye contact with their children, or they are just too busy to stop and pay attention. This says to the child, "Your ideas are not important and you yourself are of little value."

One of the more common communication problems involves telling someone else what they should think or feel. Again, this fails to value the importance of that person's emotions and thoughts. Remember Proverbs 18:13: "He who answers before listening—that is his folly and his shame."

BACK TO BASICS

Communication is behavior and healthy families have rules that govern behavior. When communicating with a child or spouse we are behaving in a certain way. If the way we behave in our communication does not show respect, then the rules governing our behavior need to be changed.

These rules should allow for comfortable communication, and for the free exchange of information back and forth with one another without fear of condemnation, coercion, manipulation, or criticism. These rules should assure everyone in the family that they will be heard and will receive a respectful response. It is important to encourage children to express themselves in a way that does not violate the rules.

Ephesians 4:26 clearly states that we will have times when we experience anger, but the verse just as clearly states that we are not to sin in our anger. Parents must obey this verse and teach their children to do so. The emotion of anger can be expressed, but in an appropriate way that falls under the rules for communication. That is, we can say, and teach our children to say, "I'm really feeling angry right now," or, "I'm hurt," or, "I'm disappointed." Such statements take ownership of feelings and acknowledge them, and yet do not blame anyone else for those feelings.

The proper expression of anger does not include yelling, sarcasm, sulking, or withdrawing in order to punish someone. These behaviors not only violate the principles of healthy communication, they increase the feeling of anger. Proverbs 15:1 instead suggests this response: "A gentle answer turns away wrath, but a harsh word stirs up anger."

Effective communication allows for respectful disagreement with the ultimate goal of resolving it. Some sample rules for good communication are:

- √ One person at a time will talk, while the others listen carefully.
- √ We will organize our own thoughts, feelings, and wants before talking.
- √ We will share these thoughts, feelings, and wants with the rest of the family.
- √ We will encourage others to communicate their thoughts, feelings, and wants to us. We will listen as they do, without criticizing.

✓ When we disagree, we will attempt to seek a mutually agreeable solution to that disagreement through negotiation.

✓ We will accept the thoughts, feelings, and wants of others without judgment or blame.

✓ We will not show disrespect for others by whining, yelling, criticizing, being sarcastic, making rude gestures, or using profanity.

✓ We will repeat what we heard the other person say to be sure that we understand correctly.

The last rule is necessary because words are emotionally charged by a person's history and experience. People may react to something that is said because they interpret the words in a way that the speaker never meant. Much miscommunication can be avoided by simply double-checking the person's meaning.

One of the main purposes of communication is to identify and resolve conflicts. This can never happen if members of the family aren't free to express themselves—respectfully, of course. Healthy families experience conflict; they learn to resolve it and train their children to do the same.

Conflict resolution involves learning to disagree with the proper attitude. Parents first need to practice the steps of conflict resolution outlined in chapter 5, and then teach their children the art of respectful negotiation.

The rules for respectful negotiation are similar to the basic rules already outlined in this chapter. Children must first demonstrate respect for their parents' authority in the way that those in a courtroom show respect for the position of the judge. Everyone present rises and acknowledges the judge's position or rank, even though the judge may later treat the proceedings very informally.

Certainly, children should not be expected to rise or salute their parents, but their attitude must be one of deference and honor. Children are then given the right to come to their parents and say, "I disagree with you. Here's what I think, here's what I feel, here's what I want."

At this point, parent-child negotiation differs from husband-wife negotiation. In husband-wife negotiation, the goal is a mutually agreeable decision. In parent-child negotiation, the parents use their God-given authority to rule on the matter at hand. Parents must be committed to following the same rules of communication that they set up for their children. They should listen respectfully and try to understand what their children are saying. Ultimately, they must decide if they are going to accept the terms of negotiation the children propose to them. Parents have the responsibility and authority to settle a matter, even though it may be in a way that their children do not appreciate or approve. Healthy families are not democracies, but *benevolent dictatorships*.

When children ask the question "Why?" parents need to separate the child's legitimate desire—to understand by seeking additional information—from a disguised challenge to the parents' authority. Children sometimes go through the negotiation process with parents, but once parents have ruled on the matter, the children refuse to let it die. Children who won't take "no" for an answer are defying the authority of their parents. Parents have a right not only to rule, but to settle the negotiations. Once this is done, discussion should cease.

LENDING AN EAR
James 1:19 echoes the need for better listening and wise speech: "My dear brothers, take note of this: Everyone should be quick to listen, slow to speak and slow to become angry." God wisely gave us two ears and only one mouth to help us carry out the instructions in this verse.

CHAPTER FOURTEEN

TEENAGE TACTICS

Parents of teenagers take note: *Adolescence is not a normal stage of development.* Of course, if you have teenagers in the house, you probably already know that. Adolescence is not universally recognized as a developmental stage. It is culturally determined and a fairly recent invention.

Nowhere does Scripture refer to adolescence as an age group, but God often used young people to carry out His plans. In 1 Timothy 4:12, Paul gives some advice to one of these young men: "Don't let anyone look down on you because you are young, but set an example for the believers in speech, in life, in love, in faith and in purity." We adults cannot ignore Paul's advice, because teenagers now play a significant part in American society.

DEFINING THE PROBLEM

The teen years, which include approximately the years from 13 to 20, carry with them some true dilemmas both for parents and teenagers. Though our society has created the rank of adolescence, it has failed to define the role in a positive way. Most Americans look at adolescence with the same mindset as the famous Greek philosopher, "Anonymous," who said, "Insanity is a genetically transmitted disease. We inherit it from our teenagers." Unfortunately, too many of us define adolescence as a time of rebellion and irresponsibility. We want our teens to act like adults, but we don't really expect it of them; therefore, we send the teens a mixed message.

The official age of adulthood varies from setting to setting. Theaters charge adult prices for teenagers who can still stay free as children in their parents' hotel room—but can't order off the children's menu in the hotel's dining room. Thus, teenagers hover somewhere between childhood and adulthood with varying privileges and responsibilities.

Teenagers themselves often seem confused about whether they want to be children or adults. Parents suffer from this same confusion. They often cannot agree on whether to launch the children from the family nest, or attempt to keep them dependent and under control for a few more years.

WHAT GOES WRONG

Normal or not, adolescence exists in our society. Parents may find it helpful to review the family life cycle and the tasks of each developmental stage, which we outlined briefly in chapter 8. Adolescence does not have to be a time of crisis for the family.

FAMILY STYLES

Families that fall into the rigid area on the circumplex often attempt to maintain tight control of a teenager. Rigid families find it difficult to make appropriate transitions. Having an adolescent in the family is definitely a transition period in parenting. If parents simply try to restrict teenage children as long as they can, the children may choose to "steal" freedom and become rebellious.

Parents of chaotic families inconsistently enforce poorly defined rules when their children are young. Their children grow up as "free spirits." Suddenly, the parents become aware of all the dangers facing teenagers. They belatedly tighten the reins and try to add some rigid controls over their teenagers' behavior. They now attempt to apply external controls at a time when the children should have already developed internal controls over their own behavior. The teens respond, somewhat appropriately, that this "is not fair." Conflict is inevitable and seldom resolved because these teens have no prior experience in respectfully negotiating with their parents.

Families that remain chaotic through the teenage years often give freedom too quickly and in chunks too large to get back if a teenager can't handle it. These families may launch their teenage children before they are equipped with the skills to successfully manage the responsibilities of adulthood. The children then often fail and return home as young adults.

We also see many families in our clinic who allow their teenage children to abuse them and their marriage by fostering the teenagers' dependence and launching them too late. The teenagers, by their codependent style of underfunctioning coupled with the parents' overfunctioning, fail to move beyond this period of their lives. This places unreasonable demands on the parents to provide financial support, food, clothing, and transportation well into their children's 20s and sometimes much older. In addition, many parents allow their teenage (and younger) children to abuse them verbally, though they would never tolerate this type of behavior from anyone else.

The onset of interest in sexuality is gradually dropping. Children are exposed daily to increased sexual stimulation in the content of movies, television, magazines, and music. AIDS education and programs to protect our children from sexual abuse also increase the sexual awareness of younger and younger children. Parents, especially those in chaotic families, may allow inappropriate exposure to sexual stimulation while still expecting their teenagers to control their impulses. However, most teenagers have not yet developed sufficient internal impulse control.

Many parents have not experienced healthy parenting during their own teenage years. They may have been sexually active as teens without their parents setting appropriate limits or assisting them to be abstinent. Now, they may not know how to help their own children with such issues. Scripture gives the example of Eli who was disciplined by God for failing to set limits and to discipline his sons in this area, even after they became young adults.

CAUSES OF REBELLION

We don't like labeling children; to label someone as "rebellious" fosters the behavior we would like to eliminate. Therefore, we try to label behavior rather than people. The symptoms we label as rebellion in teenagers don't just happen. They result from a variety of causes.

Rebellious behavior often starts long before the child reaches adolescence. A child may show defiance toward an established authority. This child may be disrespectful toward anyone in authority and may intentionally break understood rules. In addition, he may exhibit hostile-aggressive behavior toward others, or behavior that is passively aggressive. The passive-aggressive child resists authority by dawdling, or procrastinating and never finishing a task. In addition, the child may display stubbornness and forgetfulness.

The causes of rebelliousness fall into several categories. The first group were not taught respect for authority at an early age. Their misbehavior was often minimized or considered only a minor offense by their parents and was therefore overlooked. Limits were not established and no consequences were enforced to modify unacceptable behavior. Proverbs 19:18 (NASB) warns, "Discipline your son while there is hope."

Sometimes parents feel unsure about their God-given authority, or do not understand what to do to modify a child's behavior. Many parents have not worked through the leftover issues of their own childhood and cannot nurture and discipline their children as a result. If these parents were the victims of abuse or grew up in households with overly rigid parents, they may have vowed never to be as harsh to their children as their parents were to them. The parents then overcompensate and become too lenient.

Another group of children appear as second-generation victims of secular parenting books that influenced the child-rearing practices in the '60s and '70s by preaching a humanistic theology. These books taught that parents should allow children to explore, experiment, and experience life with little structure or limit-setting. In "open classroom" settings, teachers' roles became identified as "non-directive learning facilitators." Values-clarification programs in public schools, which taught that no absolute standard for morality exists, flourished during this era. It is no wonder that today's parents, raised under these influences themselves, have difficulty in teaching respect and submission to authority within their own families.

Another type of rebellion consists of those children who normally obey authority, but now struggle to exercise their growing independence in appropriate ways. Healthy growth produces a need for increasingly independent decision-making, but children need the balance of wise guidance from their parents even into young adulthood.

Some children become rebellious because their parents and other authorities provoke them through unfair treatment. Parents may have unclear expectations of their children, so that the children never know what to expect. Or a parent may send children double messages through faulty communication skills or lack of conflict resolution between parents. Some parents expect too much of their children at a young age. Others allow inconsistency and instability in the home. Physical abuse also provokes children to wrath and rebellion. Ephesians 6:4 and Colossians 3:21 both make it clear that we are not to provoke our children in this way.

Another group of children rebel because of the influence of their peers and others outside the home. The evil influences of the world become more powerful than the family. Proverbs 24:1-2 warns, "Do not envy wicked men, do not desire their company; for their hearts plot violence, and their lips talk about making trouble."

Wise parents begin early to guide their children in their choice of friends. Parents who allow freedom in dating with little guidance often learn this lesson in a painful way. At age

15 or 16, the child announces plans to marry an 18-year-old lover. Parents at this point attempt to break up the relationship and provide guidance, but with no success.

Another group of rebellious youngsters includes children who have a strong, noncompliant nature from birth. Nothing "causes" this and no one is to blame; these children are simply more inclined to rebellion by temperament. They possess an intense curiosity and tend to learn through experimentation rather than through theoretical teaching. Often, their intensity causes them to lose track of their behavior in comparison with the expected limits. These children show little awareness of how their behavior impacts other people. Though their determined nature makes them difficult children to raise, these children often grow up to be very enterprising and successful.

BACK TO BASICS
By teaching that there are moral absolutes and requiring submission to parental authority, parents prepare their children to be submissive and accountable to their Heavenly Parent as adults. Then we must let go of our children so they can be accountable to Him. This requires gradually taking our hands off our children's lives, yet staying close to offer guidance when it is needed.

CHANGING STYLES
Probably the most effective style for parenting young children falls in the structurally connected area on the circumplex. As children grow, to remain healthy, the family needs to move slowly into the flexibly detached area [see figure 22]. To accomplish this move, parents need to maintain the clear roles, rules, and consequences they have established as they begin slowly to remove the external controls of a child's behavior. This allows the child to develop and use internal controls. Parents should insist on a balanced life from their teens including: spiritual life and worship; study and education; dating; friends of the same sex; sports; hobbies; and time together as a family.

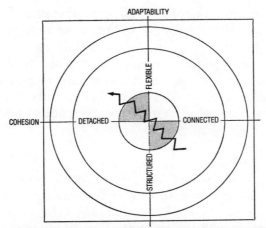

Figure 22. Circumplex Showing Movement of Ideal Family Style Through Family Cycle

Parents need to remember that they are the authority in their children's lives as long as the children live under the parents' roof. Parents have the right to take charge of their children's lives when the children are not making responsible choices for themselves. We believe it's much better to give small doses of freedom; too much freedom too quickly can be devastating, and may prove difficult to take back. With gradual increases in a child's freedom to make choices and decisions for himself, a parent can still hold the child accountable for those decisions. If the child demonstrates the ability to handle one small portion of freedom, another small portion is presented as a reward.

Parents will find it helpful to verbalize their intention and confidence in the fact that their teenagers will succeed at growing up. Teenagers need to feel that parents are on their side, supporting them as they stretch their boundaries. Let your children in on your plan for the gradual increase of their freedoms and responsibilities. Reassure them that between now and some defined endpoint your job as a parent will gradually end. This predetermined time usually occurs when the children move out of the home and become financially independent of the parents. You can then work together toward true maturity instead of pulling against each other. Your teenagers will know that they will not have to fight for every bit of freedom they can get. Once the children are out of the home, the parents then redefine their role as consultants rather than supervisors. Supervisors take responsibility for the actions of those under them; consultants merely offer suggestions *when asked,* and the recipient of that advice is not obligated to act upon it.

PREVENTING REBELLION

Preventing an attitude of rebellion starts almost at birth. Parents who do not want to face a rebellious teenager must begin raising the child to honor authority. This means becoming comfortable with the authority God grants to parents, and possibly working through any leftover issues in a parent's own childhood. Parents need to recognize that even minor childhood offenses need to be dealt with quickly, consistently, and with a loving spirit that avoids "overkill."

Children who seek to establish their independence in unacceptable or inappropriate ways need some parental guidance. Parents need to remember to remove the apron strings slowly, giving only as much freedom as each child is capable of handling in a responsible manner. Incentives, rewards, and surprises can help speed and encourage the development of responsibility. If the child does not handle the freedom properly, the parents should pull the reins back in for a while. Reassure the child and affirm that the child soon will be ready, and try again after the child has matured a little more.

Some parents provoke their teenagers to rebellion with inflexibility and refusal to listen. The only solution for this is for the parents to examine their parenting style, being humbly honest with themselves about the part they may have played in the relationship in which the rebellious behavior emerged. They then must confess their mistakes and make the changes necessary to bring their family in line with scriptural principles. The older the child, the harder it will be, but it is *never* too late to bring a child's behavior under control.

To exercise authority over outside influences in a child's

life, the parents can begin at an early age to bring their children and their children's friends together in their home. Parents should get to know their children's friends and know *about* them. Parents can then use these times for observation and as opportunities to teach their children to behave properly regardless of how others behave. Set limits on your children's behavior, and make these limits reasonable and applicable no matter where they are or who they are with. Forbidding children to be around "bad" friends sometimes evokes the natural reaction to take up for the underdog, and creates the opposite response the parent desires. Teens often defend their right to choose a particular friend by emphasizing only the friend's positive traits. Encourage children to apply equal discernment to their friends' positive and negative traits. This is especially important when teens start dating.

SURVIVING ADOLESCENCE

Raising teenagers requires a sensitive spirit, a sense of humor, and a great deal of firmness and consistency on the part of parents. If parents reflect on the emotional pain of their own teen years, they may find it easier to listen to their teens with sympathy rather than judgment. This is the time to begin letting go of your children and enjoy their emerging independence.

CHAPTER FIFTEEN

THE DISTURBED CHILD

Only in the past generation have family therapists begun to realize the truth that Scripture has stated all along. Families are systems, and in systems the sins of one generation influence and mold the thoughts and actions of the next generation. This becomes apparent when a child begins to exhibit symptoms of emotional disturbance. Traditional psychology had considered emotional difficulties to be the individual's problem. Now, we are beginning to understand that an emotionally troubled child is often a signpost for problems within the family system. As Jeremiah 31:29 puts it: "The fathers have eaten sour grapes, and the children's teeth are set on edge."

DEFINING THE PROBLEM

Dysfunctional families often manifest the characteristics of extremes on the circumplex as we discussed in chapter 3. Dysfunctions can fall into the realm of chaos, rigidity, disengagement, or enmeshment, or any combination of these.

In a dysfunctional family, all the members suffer from the stress and anxiety of the system; all experience symptoms and consequences of the dysfunction. Just as when you place stress on a chain the weakest link breaks first, when a family is under stress the weakest member is the first to show symptoms. More often than not, it is a child who first says "ouch" by developing emotional, behavioral, or psychosomatic problems. The child then may be labeled as "sick" when the actual sickness results from what is happening in the family system.

WHAT GOES WRONG

Children are susceptible to stress; they are delicate and easily develop symptoms when subjected to tension and anxiety. Each child will handle the stress in his own way, but each will, nevertheless, be affected by it. Childhood stress can be brought on by any of the extreme positions on the circumplex. Whether parents ignore their children or smother them, live in utter chaos or extreme rigidity, children bear the brunt of the dysfunction. The child often becomes the *symptom-bearer* for a family troubled by such things as alcoholism, divorce, and parental adultery.

Parents often triangulate children into a stormy or empty marriage relationship. Parents ask children to carry adult-size emotional burdens by using them as counselors and by asking them to take sides. Children don't have the ability to express or ventilate their feelings and thoughts, and they can't discern the origins of the tension they are so susceptible to. So they shoulder the burdens and may begin to show signs of emotional problems as a result of the stress they are under.

We want to emphasize here that the other family members are not to blame for the child's emotional stress. All the members of the system suffer from the same tension and anxiety. Trying to place blame on any one—or even on all—for another's emotional disturbance becomes a futile waste of time and energy. Everyone is a victim; everyone contributes to the problems of the system. And because of this, everyone is responsible for fixing the system; family health comes from a partnership among family members who are committed to overcoming dysfunction. This responsibility, however, falls most heavily on parents.

Any family dysfunction can produce a wide variety of symptoms in the individuals within that family. These symptoms can range from stomachaches and pains to reduced immunities and susceptibilities to illness. Temperament, along with the physiological and emotional makeup of individuals, helps to determine the type of symptom that a child displays. Whether a child is easy-going or intense, resistant to change or adaptable, irritable or happy-go-lucky, his basic temperament will play a part in how he handles family stress. At times, a child with a physical problem, such as allergies or asthma, may find that problem heightened by emotional stress, though the stress did not cause the original sickness. Other children who have a predisposition to hyperactivity and concentration problems may, under stress, exhibit full-blown Attention Deficit Disorder (A.D.D.) or Attention Deficit Hyperactivity Disorder (A.D.H.D.).

BACK TO BASICS

Healthy families do sometimes have troubled children. There may be a disease, an emotional problem unique to a particular child, or a cause that originated outside of the family system. However, a family with an emotionally disturbed child should not rule out the possibility that the system may contribute to the problem. If you have a child who exhibits some symptoms of emotional disturbance, no matter how slight, consider having a family evaluation done by a competent Christian family therapist. Remember, dysfunctional characteristics affect each family member whether or not they display symptoms. Ultimately, family health depends on the cooperation of each member in committing to the development of healthy family behavior.

Parents who find themselves paired with a child of a totally different temperament than their own may also find help through a family therapist. We often see parents who believe they have an emotionally disturbed child when they simply have a child whose temperament differs from their own.

REACHING OUT FOR HELP

On page 183, you will find a partial list of referral services for use in locating a competent Christian family therapist in your area. Don't be afraid to make an appointment and take a step toward family health. Your children and grandchildren and great-grandchildren will be blessed by your decision.

CHAPTER SIXTEEN

CHOSEN CHILDREN

"In love He predestined us to be adopted as His sons through Jesus Christ, in accordance with His pleasure and will" (Ephesians 1:5). How does an adopted child feel? As Christians, we should all know, for we are adopted children, chosen by God to be His. When God adopts us, He brings us into His family and makes us fellow heirs with Christ. Ephesians 1 goes on to tell us what God does for His adopted children: He gives grace, redemption, forgiveness, wisdom, and understanding. In other words, God treats His adopted children just as He treats His only begotten Son, Jesus Christ.

DEFINING THE PROBLEM

Many parents who choose to adopt seem to breeze through the process and raise happy, healthy children. Other parents face years of fear and anxiety over their adopted children. Some older, adopted children bring emotional damage with them into their new family; others may trigger emotional problems in the family system for a number of reasons. A child may be difficult to bond with; one or both parents may experience these problems in bonding. This phenomenon also occurs in natural families, but when it occurs in an adoptive family, the parents tend to believe that it is a result of adoption.

Adoptive parents often have expectations of the way their child will be. However, the child may not turn out to be the sweet, easy child that parents dreamed about rocking to sleep at night. Some children do not reciprocate affection the way parents want them to. If the adoptive parents have gone without children for several years before adopting, they may see the child as a solution to all of their life's problems. They believe that, by the child's mere presence, conflicts will resolve, and the child will "give" them joy and purpose.

Occasionally, an enmeshed family system will not accept an adopted child and the extended family members reject the child. If the child was born out of wedlock, family members may attach the label of illegitimacy to the child. We believe that there is no such thing as an illegitimate child. The biological parents may have been illegitimate in their handling of the child's birth, but the child is God's creation, and He has a purpose and plan for that child (Psalm 139).

Changing ideas about adoption and the perceived need for birth mothers and fathers—or grandparents—to be involved with the child they gave up for adoption add to the problems that adoptive parents face.

WHAT GOES WRONG
Adoptive parents face a number of fears that birth parents may not understand. Those parents who choose to adopt often live with the fear that the child's natural parents will change their minds about the adoption. Or, they face the fear that at some point in time, the child may decide to locate the natural parents and may love them more than the adoptive parents. Adoptive parents are often terrified of rejection by the child. Children seem to have a sixth sense about this fear, and may use it to get their way or to punish the parents.

Many parents, who have been unable to have children of their own, don't understand the normal behavior that occurs at times in all children, adopted or not. When their adopted child shouts, "I hate you," or, "You don't love me," the parents attribute these statements to insecurity as a result of being adopted. The parents fail to realize that these types of situations happen with all children. Because the adoptive parents are so concerned that their child love them, they have a tendency to break the rules of a healthy family system. They tolerate misbehavior and nurture excessively, treating the child with kid gloves, which, ironically, only increases any child's insecurity.

Emotional bonding and preparation for parenthood begins during pregnancy. Adoptive parents may not have the opportunity to complete this process. Consequently, they don't have as much time to prepare for the changes and adjustments that the demands of a newborn will require.

Older children who are not adopted at birth have often been abused emotionally, physically, or both. These children may be emotionally scarred by the rejection they have already faced. When you couple a child who is damaged from abuse or neglect with parents who fear rejection, the family faces a tough struggle.

Parents who are eager to adopt an older child may underestimate the depth of the wound this child may carry. Children who have been abused have a type of pseudo-maturity; they have often learned methods of self-protection that will make them difficult to handle and, at times, dangerous. Children who have suffered sexual mistreatment by a parent, prior to adoption, have learned to initiate emotional intimacy toward adults in what appears to be a sexually seductive manner. This occurs because these children confuse sexual and emotional intimacy. If this is not anticipated and prepared for, even very healthy families can experience severe problems because of the dynamics these children bring with them into the family.

Situations where "open adoption" occurs—in which the birth mother or other relatives arrange some form of contact with the child as part of the adoption agreement—present a unique challenge to establishing and maintaining the roles, rules, and boundaries necessary for a healthy family environment. When the lines of authority are not clearly presented to the child, misbehavior and rebellion against the adoptive parents may follow.

BACK TO BASICS

The need for rules, consequences, and consistency doesn't lessen in adoptive families. In fact, it may be an even stronger need where older children are concerned. All children gain a sense of security when parents apply rules and consequences with authority. Adopted children need the security of a strong healthy family with clearly defined boundaries balanced with warm expressions of affection and kindness.

Parents should take the time to learn what is and isn't normal behavior for children in the different developmental stages. Natural children come from the same womb with very different temperaments and personalities; adoption produces the same phenomenon in a family.

Bonding for an adopted child occurs in the same way as bonding for a natural child. Children bond emotionally when they feel secure in their parents' love. Once again, this security comes from setting limits and enforcing consequences, as well as sharing times of fun and intimacy as a family. This may be more difficult for the parent than the child when adopted at birth. All children need special care; adopted children do not require more than a natural child.

When an older, possibly emotionally scarred child is adopted, parents must be very patient in building a bond with the child. Older children may take a long time before they allow themselves to trust and love an adult. Parents should not get discouraged. Discouragement often causes the parent to direct their discipline at the child rather than at the child's behavior. Care should be taken to find consequences that fit the misbehavior, and never to attack the child personally. Of course, this is true of all children, whether adopted or not.

Adoption should become a household word. Parents can talk about the child being adopted even before the child is old enough to understand the term. Treating adoption as a negative thing, or hiding the fact of adoption from a child tends to put the adopted child on a different level than natural children. It may help parents to explain adoption to their children from a Christian perspective. Ephesians 6:9 tells us that "He who is both their Master and yours is in heaven, and there is no favoritism with Him." God is in control—sometimes He plans for children to stay with the mother that gave birth to them; but sometimes He has a different plan. Sometimes children are born by one parent, but God plans for them to live with another parent. Jesus, after all, was not raised by His biological Father.

A word to parents who are considering adoption: Adoptive parents experience much of the same phenomenon as natural parents when it comes to bonding and coping with their children. We often see couples who are worried about their ability to bond with an adopted child. Many times these same couples have a pet that is loved and cared for as a substitute for a child. This pet has a name, it eats with them, sleeps with them—there is a clear level of emotional bonding with the pet. But the animal didn't come from the wife's womb, and does not carry the husband's name. The couple has had no difficulty in bonding to the pet. They probably won't face much difficulty in bonding to an adopted child either.

For those couples thinking about adopting an older child, we would like to add a word of caution. Consider the risk you take in bringing an emotionally scarred child into your home. Carefully evaluate the health of your family system to see if, in fact, you are bringing this child into a strong, healthy system. If the system itself is not strong, and you bring a severely scarred child into that environment, it will tear the system apart and inflict more emotional damage on the child. We know that God has gifted some couples with the ability to handle these difficult children. Those parents have the parenting skills as well as an already established healthy system to bring those children into.

Proverbs 24:6 states, "For waging war you need guidance, and for victory many advisors." Some of these very troubled children end up producing war for their adoptive families. Our experience shows that far more of the adoptions involving older children fail than succeed. Family therapists can help couples evaluate the health of their system before potentially bringing strife into their family and adding new scars to an already troubled child.

IN THE BEGINNING
Everything written in Part 1 applies to parents of adopted children. What you model for them and teach them about family and marriage will influence their future choices of mates and parenting styles. Establishing parental authority and consistency in applying rules and consequences, coupled with patience and love, build a strong bond between any parent and child.

INSIGHTS ON COUNSELING

The decision to begin counseling is one which may have important consequences for the rest of your life. Research has shown that when individuals enter this type of treatment with a good understanding of what they are about to undertake, they are likely to achieve more favorable results.

The effectiveness of your counseling depends on a large variety of factors including the nature of the problem, the effort you put into the process, the type and length of treatment, and the therapist's skill. Nevertheless, on the average, 90 percent of all clients who continue through with their counseling sessions show significant change and improvement.

CLIENT RESPONSIBILITIES
As a client in counseling, you will have certain responsibilities. It is important for you to attend all of your scheduled appointments on time. If you are late, you will not have the benefit of a full session. Equally important are the responsibilities you have to be as active, open, and honest as possible with your therapist. Your most important responsibility, however, is to work toward the goals you and the therapist have agreed on. Seeing a therapist for 50 minutes a week will be of little benefit without additional effort outside the therapy of-

fice. This work can include thinking about the material covered in the sessions, making yourself aware of your thinking and behavior, or working on specific assignments made by your therapist.

THERAPIST RESPONSIBILITIES
The therapist will usually devote the first few sessions to assessing the types and extent of problems or concerns you have. This process requires the therapist to ask detailed questions about your history, life situations, and present distress. At times this process will involve stirring up painful or uncomfortable thoughts and feelings. Once the therapist has identified the specific problem areas, the two of you will agree upon a therapy plan including goals, methods to accomplish these goals, and approximate length of time to achieve the goals.

CONFIDENTIALITY
The client has the right to privacy concerning his or her counseling. This means that the therapist may not reveal any information about you to another person without your explicit permission. All communications and records of your treatment will be treated as private and confidential. There are some very special circumstances which are exceptions to this rule. The therapist may discuss your case with a supervisor or with other professionals clearly concerned with the case. Confidentiality will be discarded when you reveal information that indicates a clear danger of injury to yourself or others and the knowledge of abuse or neglect of a child.

HANDLING DISSATISFACTION WITH TREATMENT
It is not unusual to feel angry and upset at times about what happens in therapy. Questions or concerns about the treatment you receive should first be raised with your therapist. Explaining your thoughts and feelings, even when they are negative, is an important part of the counseling process. If, after discussing the issues with your therapist, you are still not satisfied, you have several options.

You may seek a second opinion concerning your treatment. Another approach would be to switch to a new therapist. Competent therapists recognize and accept that they will be able to serve the needs of some clients better than others.

If you believe your therapist's behavior is either unethical or does not adhere to professional standards, you again have several alternatives. You could bring the behavior to the attention of the therapist's partners, if any. Another option you may choose is to contact the appropriate state or national professional association or the state licensing or certification board.

TERMINATION

Termination should be a joint decision between you and your therapist. Too many clients terminate before all the sessions are completed. Generally, this leaves the client with unresolved issues and problems. Before terminating, speak openly and honestly with your therapist.

When all the sessions are concluded and termination is about to occur, there may be sadness, separation anxiety, or an unwillingness to give up the relationship. This is normal. Termination, to be successful, will focus on the accomplishments and success of therapy.

For help in locating a competent Christian family therapist, contact:

1. American Association for Marriage & Family Therapy
   1100 17th Street N.W., 10th Floor
   Washington, D.C. 20036
   (202) 452-0109

2. Christian Association for Psychological Studies
   CAPS International
   26705 Farmington Road
   Farmington Hills, Michigan 48018

3. Christian Family Institute
   6711 South Yale, Suite 106
   Tulsa, Oklahoma 74136
   (918) 496-3090

GLOSSARY OF
KEY TERMS

Active parenting. Planning ahead for possible behavior problems; defining the rules and consequences so that a child knows what is expected of him.

Adaptability. How a family manages change and decision-making; how roles and rules are defined; the amount of change allowed during the family life cycle.

Anniversary reaction. Emotional or physical problems occurring around the anniversary date of events that carry a profound emotional impact.

Authority. The ability to bring all the power necessary to bear on a situation to bring about a change or influence a person's behavior; limited only by the extent of one's commitment.

Balanced family. A family style that falls within the inner circle of the circumplex, avoiding the extremes of chaos, rigidity, enmeshment, and disengagement.

Boundaries. Invisible "fences" around family systems and subsystems that help to define the relationships within them; some are useful and maintain harmony and balance, some are divisive and create tension.

Chaotic. Families with no consistent leadership, frequent and dramatic role shifts, erratic discipline, rapid change, and poorly defined rules.

Circumplex. A tool developed by Dr. David Olson to measure the emotional closeness of one's family of origin and the ability of the family system to cope with change.

Codependence. A relationship characterized by an unhealthy overdependence of two people on each other which is harmful to personal growth; the maintaining of symptoms of emotional or physical addiction in a relationship.

Cohesion. The amount and extent of involvement family members have with each other; varies according to the amount of loyalty expected of family members, the amount of influence tolerated from people outside the family, and the amount of dependence between members.

Collusion. Two people acting together in secrecy against a third person, even though none of them may be aware of what they are doing or why.

Conflict resolution. Taking the steps necessary to work out the problems in a relationship and bring them to a successful solution.

Connected. A family style allowing space for friends and for personal growth; family members share activities, projects, and friends, but leave room for personal independence.

Detached. A family style in which members maintain separate, outside interests, while also working at emotional and physical intimacy.

Discipline. The development of a set of internal controls to govern behavior; communicates what to do and leads to desirable behaviors.

Disengaged. Family style showing a lack of family loyalty, high independence in decision-making, and little involvement with other family members.

Dysfunction. The impaired or incomplete functioning of a family system that produces symptoms of emotional, behavioral, or physical disorders.

Enmeshed. Family style with a high degree of loyalty to family members and overdependence on each other; characterized by everyone minding everyone else's business and an intense need to honor the family name.

Executive subsystem. The husband/wife, father/mother subsystem in a nuclear family.

Expectations. The behavior and characteristics we look for and anticipate in others.

Family of origin. The nuclear family in which an adult grew up; the family that actually reared a child.

Family system. A nuclear family group (husband, wife, and children) and the past three to seven generations in the families of both husband and wife.

Flexible. A family style that allows for change and freedom without the extreme of chaos; roles and rules are defined and stable but open to negotiation.

Flip-flop. Going to the opposite extreme of a parent's method of child raising. Same as Reactionary Parenting.

Genogram. A special kind of family tree showing each family member in relationship to the others and providing a way to examine the nature of these relationships.

Launching. Actively assisting children into adulthood careers and marriages of their own; letting go of the supervisory role of parenthood.

Leftovers. Emotional baggage from childhood; times of unresolved grief, abusive incidents, and major family crises which leave an indelible imprint on one's mind.

Life cycle. The major stages typically experienced in marriage and parenthood.

Nuclear family. A unit consisting of a mother, a father, and their children.

Nurture. The balance between unconditional love, godly training, teaching, and instructing.

Parental child. Children who carry emotional loads that are not age appropriate for them by becoming a parent's best friend, or a parent's confidant.

Pattern. The repetition of behavior and traditions through several generations of a family system, such as physical abuse, alcoholism, mental illness, sexual immorality, anger, and withdrawal.

Power. The ability to impose your will on another individual by influencing him to do something he ordinarily would not do.

Punishment. Presenting something negative or taking away something positive with the purpose of eliminating or reducing an undesirable behavior; the control is external; teaches what *not* to do in a situation.

Reactionary parenting. Going to the opposite extreme of the parenting methods used by one's own parents. Same as Flip-flop.

Reactive parenting. Reacting to undesirable behavior after it has occurred; telling the child what not to do without giving positive guidance in what to do; reacting emotionally to family events and circumstances, becoming either overprotective of children or neglecting them.

Rigid. Family style with authoritarian leadership, roles that seldom change, strict discipline, and little or no flexibility to cope with change; high expectations, unchangeable goals, and harsh punishment mark these families to varying degrees.

Roles and rules. The building blocks of a balanced family system; roles define the job each member performs in the family; rules set the guidelines for the behavior and attitudes allowed within the system.

Structured. A family style which retains well-defined roles and expectations along with unconditional acceptance; the family shares interests yet leaves room for each to grow and change as an individual.

Subsystem. Two people who share a relationship within a family system.

Transition. A time of change from one stage of the life cycle to the next.

Triangulation. Forming a triangular relationship by drawing in a third person to relieve the tension or conflict between two others.

BIBLIOGRAPHY

Marriage and Sexual Intimacy:

Carter, Les. *Dealing with the Prodigal Spouse: How to Survive Infidelity.* Nashville: Thomas Nelson Publishers, 1990.

Chesser, Barbara Russell. *21 Myths That Can Wreck Your Marriage: How a Couple Can Avoid Head-on Collisions.* Waco, Texas: Word Books, 1990.

Crabb, Lawrence J., Jr. *The Marriage Builder: A Blueprint for Couples and Counselors.* Grand Rapids: Zondervan Publishing House, 1982.

Dillow, Joseph C. *Solomon on Sex: A Biblical Guide to Married Love.* Nashville: Thomas Nelson Publishers, 1977.

Exley, Richard. *Life's Bottom Line: Building Relationships That Last.* Tulsa: Honor Books, 1990.

Harley, Willard F., Jr. *His Needs, Her Needs: Building an Affair-Proof Marriage.* Old Tappan, New Jersey: Fleming H. Revell, 1986.

Penner, Cliff and Joyce. *The Gift of Sex: The Christian's Guide to Sexual Fulfillment.* Waco, Texas: Word Books, 1981.

———. *A Gift for All Ages: A Family Handbook on Sexuality.* Waco, Texas: Word Books, 1986.

Wheat, Ed and Gaye. *Intended for Pleasure.* Revised, updated, and expanded. Old Tappan, New Jersey: Fleming H. Revell,, 1977; revised in 1981.

Wheat, Ed and Gloria Okes Perkins. *Love Life: For Every Married Couple.* Grand Rapids: Zondervan Publishing House, 1980.

Communication Skills and Conflict Resolution:

Miller, Sherod, Elam W. Nunnally and Daniel B. Wackman. *Talking Together.* Littleton, Colorado: Interpersonal Communication Programs, 1979. (A secular book.)

Miller, Sherod, Daniel B. Wackman, Elam W. Nunnally, and Phyllis A. Miller. *Connecting: With Self and Others.* Littleton, Colorado: Interpersonal Communication Programs, 1988. (A secular book.)

Wright, H. Norman. *Communication: Key to Your Marriage.* Glendale, California: Gospel Light Publications, 1974.

Family of Origin Issues:

Bloomfield, Harold H. with Leonard Felder. *Making Peace with Your Parents: The Key to Enriching Your Life and All Your Relationships.* New York: Random House, 1983. (A secular book.)

Bradshaw, John. *Bradshaw on the Family: A Revolutionary Way of Self-Discovery.* Deerfield Beach, Florida: Health Communications, 1988. (A secular book.)

Dobson, James C. *Love Must Be Tough: New Hope for Families in Crisis.* Waco, Texas: Word Books, 1983.

Forward, Susan with Craig Buck. *Toxic Parents: Overcoming Their Hurtful Legacy and Reclaiming Your Life.* New York: Bantam Books, 1989. (A secular book.)

Halpern, Howard M. *Cutting Loose: An Adult Guide to Coming to Terms with Your Parents.* New York: Bantam Books, 1977. (A secular book.)

Huskey, Alice. *Stolen Childhood: What You Need to Know about Sexual Abuse.* Downers Grove, Illinois: InterVarsity Press, 1990.

Wright, H. Norman. *Making Peace with Your Past.* Old Tappan, New Jersey: Fleming H. Revell, 1985.

Codependent Relationships:

Hemfelt, Robert, Frank Minirth, and Paul Meier. *Love Is a Choice: Recovery from Codependent Relationships.* Nashville: Thomas Nelson Publishers, 1989.

Hemfelt, Robert and Paul Warren. *Kids Who Carry Our Pain: Breaking the Cycle of Codependency for the Next Generation.* Nashville: Thomas Nelson Publishers, 1990.

Quick, Daryl E. *The Healing Journey: For Adult Children of Alcoholics.* Downers Grove, Illinois: InterVarsity Press, 1990.

Family Life Cycle and Parenting:

Curran, Dolores. *Traits of a Healthy Family: Make Your Family Stronger, Happier, and More Fulfilled.* New York: Ballantine Books, 1983. (A secular book.)

Dobson, James C. *Dare to Discipline.* Wheaton, Illinois: Tyndale House Publishers, 1971.

_____ *Preparing for Adolescence.* Ventura, California: Regal Books, 1978.

_____ *The Strong-Willed Child.* Wheaton, Illinois: Tyndale House Publishers, 1979.

_____ *Hide and Seek.* Old Tappan, New Jersey: Fleming H. Revell, revised 1991.

Huggins, Kevin. *Parenting Adolescents.* Colorado Springs, Colorado: NavPress, 1989.

Kesler, Jay, ed. *Parents and Teenagers: A Guide to Solving Problems and Building Relationships.* Wheaton, Illinois: Victor Books, 1985.

Kesler, Jay, Ronald Beers, and LaVonne Neff, eds. *Parents and Children: A Guide to Solving Problems and Building Relationships.* Wheaton, Illinois: Victor Books, 1986.

Narramore, Bruce. *Help! I'm a Parent.* Grand Rapids: Zondervan Publishing House, 1972.

Divorce, Remarriage, and Adoption:

Bustanoby, Andre. *But I Didn't Want a Divorce.* Grand Rapids: Zondervan Publishing House, 1978.

_____ *The Ready-Made Family: How to Be a Stepparent and Survive.* Grand Rapids: Zondervan Publishing House, 1982.

Hart, Archibald D. *Children and Divorce: What to Expect. How to Help.* Waco, Texas: Word Books, 1982.

Strom, Kay Marshall. *Chosen Families: Is Adoption for You?* Grand Rapids: Zondervan Publishing House, 1985.

Swihart, Judson J. and Steven L. Brigham. *Helping Children of Divorce: Practical Suggestions for Parents and Relatives, Friends, and Teachers.* Downers Grove, Illinois: InterVarsity Press, 1982.

Genograms:

Marlin, Emily. *Genograms: The New Tool for Exploring the Personality, Career, and Love Patterns You Inherit.* Chicago, Illinois: Contemporary Books, 1989. (A secular book.)

McGoldrick, Monica and Randy Gerson. *Genograms and Family Assessment.* New York: W.W. Norton & Company, 1985. (A secular book.)

Introduction to Family Therapy:
Posterhaus, James. *Counseling Families: From Insight to Intervention.* Grand Rapids: Zondervan Publishing House, 1989.
Wynn, J.C. *The Family Therapist: What Pastors and Counselors Are Learning from Family Therapists.* Old Tappan, New Jersey: Fleming H. Revell, 1987.